C000258289

Please Yourself

Please Yourself

How to Stop People-Pleasing and Transform the Way You Live

Emma Reed Turrell

4th ESTATE • *London*

4th Estate
An imprint of HarperCollins*Publishers*
1 London Bridge Street
London SE1 9GF

www.4thEstate.co.uk

HarperCollins*Publishers*
1st Floor, Watermarque Building, Ringsend Road
Dublin 4, Ireland

First published in Great Britain in 2021 by 4th Estate

2

Copyright © Emma Reed Turrell 2021

Emma Reed Turrell asserts the moral right to be identified
as the author of this work in accordance with the
Copyright, Designs and Patents Act 1988

A catalogue record for this book is
available from the British Library

ISBN 978-0-00-840937-1 (hardback)
ISBN 978-0-00-840938-8 (trade paperback)

All rights reserved. No part of this publication may be
reproduced, stored in a retrieval system, or transmitted,
in any form or by any means, electronic, mechanical,
photocopying, recording or otherwise, without the
prior permission of the publishers.

This book is sold subject to the condition that it shall not, by
way of trade or otherwise, be lent, re-sold, hired out or otherwise
circulated without the publisher's prior consent in any form of
binding or cover other than that in which it is published and
without a similar condition including this condition being
imposed on the subsequent purchaser.

Set in Dante MT Std
Printed and bound in Great Britain by
CPI Group (UK) Ltd, Croydon

MIX
Paper from
responsible sources
FSC
www.fsc.org   FSC™ C007454

This book is produced from independently certified FSC™ paper
to ensure responsible forest management.

Find out more about HarperCollins and the environment at
www.harpercollins.co.uk/green

To Thomas and Elsa, please yourselves.

Contents

Introduction

We all know a people-pleaser. Perhaps they struggle to say what they want, or they don't like to go against the grain. They might say sorry when they've done nothing wrong or feel guilty for changing plans. Someone who finds it easier to say yes than to explain why not. Maybe they do all these things. Maybe it's you?

I used to be a people-pleaser. Born with characteristic punctuality on the morning of my due date, I was a child who was good at making people happy. I'd relish the opportunity to entertain if my parents had a party and willingly visit old people's homes to sing them carols at Christmas. Ever the chameleon, I could adapt myself to fit into any social situation and use my pleasing powers to give people what they wanted. As an adult, I still found myself doing it at work and with friends, prioritising other people's happiness and seemingly unable to say no. I was avoiding the risk of someone disliking me (in reality, I was avoiding the risk of disliking myself) but people-pleasing was stopping me living authentically and, at times, even making me ill. I do it a lot less now and I feel a lot better for it.

In my clinical practice as a psychotherapist I see people every day who are wrestling with the complicated dilemmas of a life in which you can't please everyone but you don't yet have permission to please yourself. We work together to help them to come to the liberating realisation that there is no pleasing some people, so the trick is to stop trying.

Recovering people-pleasers can look back with twenty-twenty hindsight and say, 'I wish I'd known then what I know now'. That pleasing yourself isn't actually saying, 'Me first', it's simply saying, 'Me too'.

This book has been written to help you know *now* what you'll know then.

So, I'd like to talk to you about people-pleasing ... if that's OK?

Why do we do it?

You might have been told that people-pleasing is about being thoughtful, or considerate, or kind. In reality it's about a desire to organise the reactions of other people and avoid the discomfort their dislike brings up in you. People-pleasing is a strategy designed to keep you safely in control, wrapped up in a veneer of pseudo-generosity or flexibility.

People-pleasers can't bear to disappoint, and to be disliked feels crippling. We fear being judged and found to be wanting. Feeling needed feels a lot like feeling loved. We do it because we're afraid of losing people and yet we lose ourselves in our futile bid to keep them happy.

The origins of the people-pleaser's behaviour are understandable. To be disliked would be dangerous to a pack animal such as ourselves, dependent on the group for fire, food and protection. Fear, guilt and shame are primal feelings, designed to keep us safely on the inside of a group. Don't do anything that might cost you your place by the fire and get you exiled into the wilderness, to die of exposure or at the claws of a hungry predator. Don't do anything unacceptable if the punishment could be death. However, these feelings have not evolved in the way that modern life has. Today I see people in my therapy room who are guilty of crimes as abhorrent as forgetting a birthday, calling in sick, or cancelling a friend for dinner. For doing *anything* that has an impact on anyone else or anything that might make someone feel discomfort. One people-pleaser I knew arrived late to a session one week, more flustered than usual, having been delayed by an aggressive charity fundraiser, drawn into an unwanted conversation about the Second Coming, and signed up for a subscription to an online language school, all on her way from the car park and all because she couldn't bear to say no. 'They see me coming!' she wailed. These primal feelings of guilt and shame were designed to be deeply painful, and avoided at all costs, yet they are attached to actions today that no longer warrant their acerbic whip. Without updating our understanding of these primal feelings, we can find ourselves avoiding any and all upset, even when we're not the ones at fault.

People-pleasing isn't a quirk of character, it's a product of conditioning. Within these pages we will explore the development of the people-pleaser, from birth, through childhood and adolescence, and into adulthood, where those early beliefs get reinforced through the choices they make today.

The darker side of people-pleasing

Historically, people-pleasing has often been labelled a female affliction, and there is truth in the cultural stereotype that girls are raised to be quiet and to put others first. But people-pleasing today is a problem for everyone, regardless of gender or age or status. For too long it has been reported breezily as a problem of being 'easy-going' or 'too nice'. Its write-up has been light and even playful. Its treatment has been flippant and dismissive – 'just don't worry what other people think'. Or it's been weaponised into the philosophy of not giving a fuck, in which we're encouraged to dismiss the haters or 'let that shit go', when really we need to give that shit our full attention and deal with it decisively. If it was as simple as not caring we'd have all done it by now.

It isn't. People-pleasing is a self-sacrificing behavioural compulsion. And it is as damaging for the people we please as for the pleasers themselves. People-pleasing isn't a benign habit to learn to live with, a foible full of good intentions. It's anxiety in action. It's the fear of something you can't control, namely other people's emotions. Pleasers will go to great lengths to hide their truth, to avoid having an impact or causing upset. Unchecked, this urge to please, or not displease, can result in anxiety and depression, poor physical health, low self-worth and dangerous self-abandonment.

Today there are more people than ever to please. In our busy, modern lives the pleasing domain feels limitless, our roles and responsibilities are sprawling and boundaries are undefined. We're expected to be flexible at work and instantly accessible to friends, to tag-team with partners or sandwich-care for young children and ageing parents, without ever clocking off. Social networks have put people-pleasers in front of infinite online audiences, outsourcing their self-esteem to marketing algorithms and the twitchy thumbs of strangers.

You might not consider yourself a people-pleaser. Many of my clients start from this position, seemingly unencumbered by the opinions of others and ready to run their own race independent of anyone else. The most obvious people-pleasers may well be the ones who are actively making life easier and more comfortable for those around them, but they are only the tip of the iceberg and people-pleasing can come in many forms, wearing many disguises. Different relationships with the pressure to please can elicit a range of reactions, including consciously *not* pleasing in an effort to be autonomous, but all are defences against the same sense of low self-worth, lack of power and fear of rejection. In the next chapter I'll introduce you to the four different types of people-pleaser, all with a version of the same problem: an inability to feel good enough just as they are.

Yet there is another way. Not a selfish way but a way to be free to respond to our needs as well as those of others. Being liked, or needed, is not all it's cracked up to be if it means we sacrifice ourselves in the process, and at some point we all have a choice to make: whether to be a people-pleaser or an authentic person.

To please yourself is actually the more responsible and generous way to engage in relationships. From here we can be more authentic and more respectful, with the resources and ability to help others as well as ourselves, because giving ourselves more of our attention doesn't take it away from someone else. It's not pie.

Care better, not less

This book offers the alternative to people-pleasing. But it's not a message of caring less; in fact, it calls for caring more and caring better. Caring *more* genuinely, *more* fairly, *more* appropriately and *more* consistently, for yourself *and* for others. Caring enough to take the risk that the real you won't be acceptable to some, in order to experience unconditional acceptance from others. Caring enough not to saddle someone else with the unwanted responsibility of being your judge and executioner. Caring enough to acknowledge that we cannot truly say yes unless we can also say no. Saying yes is meaningless if no was never really an option.

This book will help you get better at being disliked, instead of staying quiet. It will equip you to recover instead of fearing failure. It will teach you how to accept judgment instead of avoiding it. I won't show you a way to stop people-pleasing without upsetting anyone, but I will show you that being less likeable is both survivable and positively thrive-able. Because any relationship that couldn't withstand a conversation about your needs and feelings wasn't stable to begin with and, moreover, it was occupying the space of one that could.

Please Yourself seeks to explain and reframe our original motivations for people-pleasing and offer hope for a way forward in which we can stand down from taking care of someone else, and get on with the task of taking care of ourselves. We can learn that people's reactions to us are more of a reflection of the relationship they have with themselves than a legitimate judgment of us. We can learn to tune in to our feelings and needs and notice that, if we feel resentful, that's our cue to set a boundary with the person we resent.

This book will teach you how to be you. It will teach you how to stop chasing people and start attracting them instead, trusting that what belongs to you will come to you easily and what doesn't was never yours to begin with. It will motivate you to spend time with the people who fit your future, not your past. It will make you a better friend, partner, child and parent. It will help you care better for others, without taking on their problems, through caring better for yourself.

And this book will prepare you for loss. Because with growth, inevitably there is loss. There will be those who don't want you to stop pleasing. But when they tell you that 'you've changed', you'll know that what they're really saying is, 'I don't like that you're no longer doing it *my* way'.

The many faces of people-pleasing

We will journey through the stories and lives of people-pleasers I have encountered, offering a behind-the-scenes therapy perspective on the parent-pleasers (and the pleasing parents), the pleasing friends, the people-pleasers at work and many more. The examples within these pages are based on hundreds of people-pleasers I have worked with, across different therapy services and over many years of clinical practice. Their names and identifying details have been changed to maintain confidentiality, and any similarities to individuals are purely coincidental. In some cases, stories from a number of sources have been merged to further protect identities, but the experiences remain real, the meaning is true and their learning is our lesson if we choose to listen. Whether you're a parent or not, in a relationship or not, a man or a woman, or however you identify, I'd encourage you to read all the stories and see which ones resonate with you and what you can learn that might help you. Within every chapter there will be reflective questions, insights and techniques that can help you understand yourself more deeply and point you towards a different, better way. By the end, you'll have a complete handbook to Please Yourself.

Your empathy is a gift. When we people-please we cast our care indiscriminately before those who won't or can't appreciate it. When we please ourselves, we give other people the permission to do the same. This book will teach you how to direct your care at the people who merit it most, starting with yourself.

The Four Pleasing Profiles

Although many of us might initially recognise ourselves in the over-apologiser, the employee who hates to call in sick, or the last person to serve themselves at dinner, our motivations for people-pleasing will differ. Through thousands of client hours in my clinical practice, I've identified four different types of people-pleasing and created four pleasing profiles.

The Classic people-pleaser

I call the more 'traditional' people-pleasers the Classics. They take pride in their ability to get things right, choosing the ideal birthday gift or hosting the perfect dinner party. No doubt they'll be really good at it and part of their reward system will come from the appreciation and accolade that they receive from the people they please. This becomes their definition of themselves. It's who they are and why they exist, to make life easier and more comfortable for other people. Ask them what *they* want and they'll draw a blank.

They crave the hit they get from skilfully inhabiting someone else's world and basking in the warmth reflected back at them. That moment of being special to someone else is more compelling that anything they could ever hope to give to themselves. Their self-esteem has been replaced by 'others-esteem' and they're only good enough if you say so. A pat on the head from an authority figure feels like winning the lottery for a Classic pleaser.

The Shadow people-pleaser

Shadows expect to live in service of other people who occupy the light, those who are seemingly more important and more worthy of the world's attention.

Somewhere in the Shadow's early life there was probably a narcissist, a person who lacked empathy and expected admiration from others. Around this energy, the Shadow pleaser worked out how to stay in favour by deflating themselves and inflating the other. They worked out how to be the best support act or the perfect wingman, somebody's number one Number Two.

The way Shadows see the world is that the other person's need is greater than their own; they're the first to give up their seat on the bus and are forever holding open the door. As adults, they continue to seek out opportunities to bolster the egos of other people. They gravitate towards status and success in others and make fantastic groupies. But they are only satisfied being your number one fan, which can result in some pretty competitive people-pleasing among groups of Shadows and, considering how hard they try to win your affection, they can make for a difficult friend to have. Sometimes vying for the *best* friend title becomes more important than being a good friend in the first place, and jealous Shadows can quickly become paranoid and destructive. When one offers to give you their jacket, another has to volunteer a kidney. You are more of a prize than a person and you can feel more like their trophy than their friend.

The Pacifier people-pleaser

People-pleasing can sometimes be more about a fear of getting it wrong than a desire to get it right.

The Pacifier is an example of a pleaser who operates primarily from a 'don't displease' position. They are the social glue that keeps situations amicable and they facilitate collaboration. They are inclusive and amenable. Like the conductor of an orchestra, they task themselves with the job of bringing individuals together to a place of harmony, while taking up no space themselves. If you were to cut a Pacifier they would bleed breezy indifference. After apologising for bleeding everywhere, of course.

Growing up, the Pacifier may not have felt it was safe to upset someone else or to be around discord. These pleasers learned how to placate and pacify by soothing the strong feelings of others, or by burying their own feelings to avoid provoking a hostile reaction. Pacifiers also develop in families where another child has reserved the role of chief boat-rocker. If one child is defiant and confronting, it's not uncommon for their sibling to fall into a Pacifier pattern to steady the ship.

The Pacifier is the Goldilocks of the pleasing profiles, seeking out the bland acceptability of the middle of the road. Neither too much of this nor too little of that, they occupy the common ground, never voicing a contentious opinion or a preference that might be unpopular.

The Resistor people-pleaser

These are the underground people-pleasers – the ones who wouldn't identify themselves as pleasers at all.

This is someone who can't tolerate people being displeased with them but, unlike the other pleasing profiles, the Resistor's defences result when they realise that they can't (or won't) do what it takes to elicit a favourable reaction. Unable to behave in a way that would ever be pleasing enough to prevent criticism or rejection, the Resistor's only remaining defence is to exit the game. After all, if you don't play then you can't lose.

As adults, Resistors will avoid intimacy in relationships and only engage at arm's length, their soft underbelly protected by a persona that appears immune to criticism whilst simultaneously closed off to connection. Their artificially thickened skin makes them impervious to the judgment of others, both good and bad. They shut off their feelings in order to escape the pain of failure. Self-sufficient, you might see them keep their distance in groups or take a role as leader. Somewhere between confident and dismissive, they appear to have the courage of their convictions and are not easily influenced, nor are they easily praised or comforted in times of trouble.

They might not look like the more traditional people-pleasers, but they share in a pathological reaction to the pressures to please. They feel the same weight of judgment but, unable to tolerate it, they learn to ignore it, resist it or deny its existence. And they may not always be aware that this is even happening, which can make it harder to help them. Often alerted by substance misuse, depression, burnout or divorce, the Resistor first has to acknowledge their well-masked relationship with the pressures to please, before they can move to a healthier place of pleasing themselves.

You might recognise yourself in one of these profiles, or in more than one. You might even notice aspects of all of them in the ways you behave and in the people-pleasers you know. Over a lifetime we will lean on the strategies of different profiles at different times, all with the same intention, to defend ourselves against the risk of rejection.

Whatever your relationship with pleasing people, in the pages that follow you will meet examples of the four pleasing profiles and discover the lessons they learned along the way that helped them become more aware, and better equipped, to make authentic and fulfilling connections.

Let's begin by looking at how a people-pleaser is created, based on the messages we received as children.

The early people-pleaser

I come from a family of diehard football fans. I had my first season ticket at a young age and would trail dutifully through the turnstiles at Fratton Park every other Saturday behind my grandfather, my father and my older brother. I wanted to go, if only for the sausage rolls and chocolate bars that would appear from Grandad's coat pockets at half-time, but the actual football didn't really interest me at the time. I used to take a book to amuse myself while the crowds around me leaped out of their seats to cheer and heckle. My dad recounts how I would look up from the pages from time to time to enquire how long was left. When he asked, 'Why's that, aren't you enjoying the game?' I would answer, with all the transparent cunning of a six-year-old, 'I'm just having *such* a good time that I'd like to know how much longer I have left to enjoy it.' I might not have been all that convincing in hindsight, but I wanted to answer my dad in a way that would make him happy. I didn't want him to feel disappointed or for him to think I'd rather be somewhere else. I guess he didn't want to disappoint me either, as he never once suggested I might not quite be telling the truth.

Young children are built to please and it starts as early as six weeks old, when babies first develop the ability to smile. Not because they feel happy exactly but because of the reaction they get from the person they smile at. Smile at their caregiver and they get played with, cuddled, sung to and tickled, in essence a smile gets them loved. Even a tiny baby has an awareness that they need this love in order to survive, and evolution has granted them a superpower – the power to please.

As we grow up and become more self-sufficient, we still need relationships to thrive but, biologically at least, we are less dependent on other people for our survival. What happens then, when the pack we're raised by determines that we need to remain pleasing and subservient, that those early pleasing smiles and adaptations weren't a route to independence and unconditional love, but instead were set to become our identity?

I believe that parents typically do the best that they can with what they have but there will always be blind spots; they can't give you what they didn't get themselves or didn't know to be missing. If children pick up signals that they need to pay more attention to their parents' needs than their own, unchecked they may develop into people-pleasers. I use the term 'parents' here but I'm referring to any adult who was responsible for taking care of you; it could include aunts and uncles, grandparents, foster carers, teachers or older siblings. Wherever you got your messages, spoken or unspoken, about how to be in the world.

Let's look at the story of one of my clients, Bianca, to get an insight into the creation of a people-pleaser.

Bianca

Bianca would rush into our therapy sessions carrying multiple bags laden with stuff for multi-tasking days in service of other people, arms and calendar impossibly full.

As a child, she could never shake the feeling that she wasn't doing enough or being enough for her mother, who would spend her days in bed and barely noticed Bianca. Looking back, Bianca could see her mother had been depressed; years of trying for a baby had taken their toll on her and even the arrival of a baby daughter at long last couldn't lift the dark cloud that filled the house. Bianca was an only child and she dedicated her early life to pleasing her parents in any way she could, trying hard to meet her mother's expectations and earn her father's praise, and jettisoning her own needs along the way.

Sowing the seeds of people-pleasing

If a parent is depressed or anxious, it can feel safer for a child to look for ways to keep them happy, to keep them regulated and help them manage their distress. Taking care of a parent's feelings and needs might mean you have to give up on your own. You might set up a chain reaction in which you take care of other people's needs and require them to do the same for you. Perhaps you expect your own child to please you now or perhaps it's a friend or partner. Everyone is kept busy pleasing someone else but no one is truly pleasing themselves.

Bianca believed her mother when she found fault in her, and she accepted her mother's lack of love as what she deserved. Children typically aren't able to see their parents as flawed and, if a mistake is made, it's counter-intuitively easier for a child to file it as their own failing. They keep their parent 'perfect' because, if a parent can't be relied upon to get it right, what hope does the child have? Except that, of course, parents *do* make mistakes and these need to be spelled out to a child, owned by the parent and appropriately repaired, so that the child doesn't take away a misplaced sense of responsibility. Maybe you notice that your parents weren't quick to apologise when they made a mistake, and perhaps you took responsibility for more than was appropriate; perhaps you still do.

If something traumatic happens to a child in early life, their best bet may be to create rules for themselves to help them feel more in control, a set of 'dos and don'ts' that they can follow to gain a sense of safety in their world. The rules they apply might be way off the mark in reality but they give the child an option for order within chaos. If this was the case for you, perhaps conflict felt catastrophic and that led you to create rules around pleasing other people. We can acknowledge that this was a trauma response made for good reason at the time but recognise that it might no longer be so necessary or helpful to you now.

Bianca's father adored her mother and Bianca watched him pander to her every need. Her mother could be cruel to him in return but he would always be ready and willing to apologise and restore peace in the house. He was a people-pleaser himself, and Bianca picked up some of her people-pleasing patterns from him. As children we learn from what our parents do, as well as what they say. If your parent put themselves at the bottom of the pile, as Bianca's father usually did, the chances are you've learned to do the same. If your parent was engaged in pleasing some other 'parent' – real or imaginary – keeping one eye on you and the other eye on the expectations of others, you may have learned to follow suit. If they cared too much about what other people thought, you might find that you care too much as well.

Bianca's father would praise her for being a 'good girl' and keeping her mother happy, grateful no doubt to be able to share the load with someone else and in this way at least, Bianca felt important and needed. Children soak up praise. If you were good at entertaining the grown-ups or you always let the other children take their turn first, you were probably praised for it. The more you were praised for being funny or kind or generous or patient, the more you might have sought out these situations again and the more this might have become part of your emerging identity.

Cultivating a perennial pleaser

Bianca dedicated her early life to earning her mother's approval and trying to please her, to validating her wishes and supporting her needs, but even when she moved out and could begin her own life, nothing changed. She had learned to manage her mother's feelings by having none of her own and, when she finally left home, she found herself continuing those pleasing patterns. She married a man who was critical and dismissive of her and yet she still sought to please him, turning a blind eye to his drinking and the extra-marital affairs.

Decades passed and eventually she came to counselling. 'I know I'm not right,' she told me, 'but I don't know what's wrong.' She knew she was depressed but she didn't know why. As she saw it, she enjoyed her job, she had good friends and she kept herself busy with her grandchildren. In reality, she had tried to keep away from her own problems by helping others with theirs and she'd completely lost touch with her needs – if indeed she'd ever known them.

Our job was to piece together her sense of self, beginning with her abandoned feelings.

Feeling your way out of pleasing

Feelings are crucial to pleasing yourself; they tell you what's right or wrong about a situation and steer you towards the appropriate course of action. People-pleasers like Bianca often end up not feeling anything at all, or only feeling other people's feelings; or they muddle one feeling up with another and are left confused about what action to take.

If your family didn't 'do' feelings, you might have learned to fit into your tribe by muting your feelings too. Anger? What anger? If you don't pick up on the sensation in the first place, you won't be able to act on it or meet the need it's communicating. Alcohol anaesthetises pain, depression flattens feelings, and overworking provides distraction. Be curious about how feelings were avoided in your family and how you avoid your own feelings now. Maybe you were encouraged to be pragmatic and unemotional, so you look only for solutions and always try to 'fix', even when it comes to matters of the heart.

Maybe your family upheld a gender stereotype, for example 'boys don't cry' or 'girls are sweet', or a cultural message like the British stiff upper lip, or an age-related rule such as 'children should be seen and not heard'. If so, your feelings options might have been delimited for you before you were even born.

Maybe you got a message that only certain feelings are justifiable, for instance if your mother worried about everything, or your father raged on the roads. In that environment you might pick up that one feeling fits all and a single blanket approach is appropriate to every situation. You worry about things when you should be making a change. You rage against your circumstances when you must accept what is. You feel *something* but it's not the right response, so whatever action you take is redundant and you never feel relief.

Maybe it was your job to look after your entire family's emotions, to keep things on an even keel or be the ray of sunshine who cheered everybody up. You were so busy tuning into what *they* needed that you didn't take the time to tune in to yourself.

Feel for yourself

In our sessions, Bianca and I went back to revisit some of her earlier experiences, this time with the full complement of feelings that she didn't have access to at the time.

One of her most heartbreaking memories was of lunchtimes at her junior school when she was about eight years old. Her friends would all arrive with smart plastic lunchboxes, complete with a handle like a little square suitcase, decorated with pictures of popular cartoon characters and perfectly labelled with their names printed in their mothers' neat letters. 'I never had a lunchbox,' Bianca told me, 'it was always a tatty old bag from the supermarket and I remember I'd keep it on my lap so that nobody would notice.' Tears welled in her eyes as she went on, 'I used to cobble together my own lunch every morning. I remember the butter was always too cold and it would tear the bread and my yoghurt would burst in the bag and end up all over my books. If I had milk left over from breakfast I'd take that to drink, but I never knew you had to keep it cold, so it was always sour by lunchtime.' Her friends would lay out their food on the table and Bianca would stare wide-eyed at the care and attention that had gone into the preparation of their picnics: jam sandwiches cut up into different shapes, miniature boxes of raisins, chocolate biscuits in shiny foil wrappers and cartons of fruit juice with a straw. 'It makes me want to cry when I think about it now,' she said. 'Their mums had done that for them. My mum hadn't even got out of bed that week.'

Bianca's depression had so far defended her against her sadness but it was time to bring her feelings back online and use them to help her reflect on her memories with a new-found compassion for the child who had survived them.

Acting on your feelings

Acknowledging how we feel is just the beginning for the recovering people-pleaser. Then it's about what we do with the information our feelings provide. With her feelings now available to her, Bianca could begin to reflect on what she'd needed back then and what reparative action she needed to take in the present.

What if we don't have a model for taking action to meet our own needs? When we were babies we all had to rely on someone else to meet our needs: we would cry to elicit a change in state, we would smile and giggle to show appreciation and get more of what we wanted. But as adults, with all of our sophisticated communication skills and resources, what if we still find ourselves seeking to please (or not displease) someone else, in an attempt to get our feelings resolved for us? Even if Bianca had understood how sad she'd felt at the time, she wouldn't have known what to do about it. She wasn't even sure how to help herself now.

As with our feelings, our ability to act can be curbed by the messages we received when we were growing up. Before we could help her take the right steps now, we had to find out how Bianca unconsciously hobbled her attempts to act on her feelings.

What gets in your way?

If you know how you feel, but you weren't allowed to take action for yourself, you might have to try to get someone else to take it for you now. Perhaps you weren't encouraged to try things or to take risks, or you were told off when you asked directly for what you wanted, or challenged your parents' point of view. Perhaps your parents did everything for you or made every decision on your behalf. You can't ask directly for what you need so you've learned to hint, or pout, or flatter or plead. You have to coerce somebody into changing the situation for you or give up on change altogether.

Maybe nobody ever taught you how to take action. You don't know how to stand up for yourself, so you wouldn't know what to do with the feeling of anger even if you could acknowledge it. Maybe you didn't see your parents take action, perhaps they were passive and seemed resigned to their lot in life. Instead of changing the situation, you try to change yourself and look for ways to not mind so much.

If you don't believe change is possible or you don't believe you can make a difference, either because you've never experienced getting what you want or because you don't believe you deserve a different outcome, you might give up your agency in the process. You'll work hard for other people instead, accepting what's on offer and feeling grateful for what you get.

You might have been taught to take the wrong action. Maybe you were told to 'rise above it' or 'turn the other cheek' when someone treated you badly, instead of standing up for yourself or pushing back. Maybe you were told not to bring people down when you were sad, so you still hide your tears today.

Taking the wrong action, or no action at all, is like reaching for a glass of water when you're hungry, or trying to deny the rumbling in your stomach because it isn't time for lunch. Bianca tried to take her pleasure from keeping other people happy, or persuade herself that she had nothing to be depressed about, but these weren't the actions that were required and they couldn't hit the spot.

Bianca's pleasing profile

Bianca was a blend of the pleasing profiles, set on taking care of as many people as she could. She would Classic please her friends and family, saying yes to everything and coming up with endless ways to make people happy. She would martyr herself for those she saw as superior and live out a life of servitude, like the Shadow. She used Pacifier patterns to keep the peace at home, around a husband who had unpredictable moods, and she hated to let anybody down, running herself ragged to keep up with her list of never-ending commitments.

If she'd ever given up on trying to connect with her mother, or had lost faith in her efforts to please, she might have developed into a Resistor and cut her losses by now, not free of the pressure to please but at least able to mitigate it by avoiding relationships in general. I did see her dip into these Resistor patterns at times, in the numbness and detachment that would take over during a bout of particularly deep depression. It's possible that her mother had been a Resistor too, reliant on her depression to mask her own vulnerability.

Different combinations of environmental factors will create different blends of the pleasing profiles, which can shift and evolve over time. Perhaps you can notice your pleasing profile in your beginnings and then think about how you show up in relationships today.

Repairing the people-pleaser

In our sessions, Bianca came to understand how her inner people-pleaser had been created in response to her mother's emotional unavailability and the template she'd received from her people-pleasing father. As an adult, her task was to now become emotionally available to herself, to pay attention to her feelings and to act on what she needed in terms of self-care and support. Some weeks into our work together, she came to a session and told me she'd just seen a beautiful 'back to school' display in the window of a gift shop on the high street. As she was talking, she reached into her bag and produced two brightly coloured lunchboxes with matching drinks bottles, one for her granddaughter and one for herself. She couldn't stop the tears as she showed me this emerging part of her, a part who was finally learning to please herself.

Understanding why we do what we do can offer us an opportunity for change. Through the stories of clients like Bianca, I will take you behind the scenes to look at the origins of the people-pleaser, the impact people-pleasing had on their lives and the lives of those around them, and the lessons they learned that helped them to embark on a journey of pleasing themselves. We'll look at the lessons and the learnings for you too and help you to ask yourself those 'therapy'-type questions that can bring your feelings into your awareness and point you towards the actions you might need to take to feel more satisfied in your own life.

Realising what was missing back then shows us what we need to seek today. Once you can spot the wounds from which your people-pleasing developed, the task becomes yours to heal them if you choose to. You may have been failed in the past but, if you collude with the original conditions and continue to discount your needs now, *you* fail yourself in the present.

We can repair the damage. Every time we hear and act on our feelings in an authentic way, we give ourselves the message that we matter. We create a new pathway where we have permission to feel, our feelings are valid and we can take meaningful action to resolve them. The more we experience the positive outcomes of acting on our feelings, the more likely we will be to do it again and the loop becomes a virtuous circle.

Throughout the chapters to come, I'll invite you to reflect on your own beginnings and behaviours. Take your time with the questions and exercises that appear (you may wish to have a paper and pen to hand) and see if you can let yourself be curious about where you've come from and what's made you who you are today.

The birth of your people-pleaser

Take a moment to remember the messages you got when you were growing up.

Can you identify the origins of your people-pleaser?

Maybe you were praised for your pleasing behaviours.
The thank-you letters you wrote, your willingness to share,
your reputation for being sensible or sweet, or for being a
'good' baby or a 'kind' sibling. Perhaps your identity was
tied up with being easy-going, hard-working, amenable,
or sociable, and maybe your parents were the same. Or
maybe you learned to not displease – perhaps it didn't feel
OK to disappoint people at home or at school. Perhaps
negative emotions felt unsafe, perhaps one or more of
your caregivers was quick to anger, or perhaps one of your
siblings had already reserved the role of rebel. You may
have been encouraged to think instead of feel, to be
rational instead of emotional. You may have learned how
not to rock the boat or cause conflict, how to fly under the
radar or keep the peace, to disappear or play second fiddle.

Now that you have a sense of how you became a
people-pleaser, see if you can notice something about *why*
it might have happened.

What can you notice now, as an adult, that you didn't know back then?

See if you can notice what else was going on for your
parents and caregivers, what you know about their situation
at the time and where they came from. Realising that your
mother was a chronic people-pleaser or that your father was
a perfectionist won't undo the pressure they placed on you
but it can go some way to understanding that this was *their*
way, not *the* way. You can use this awareness to do things

differently now. Drop the inter-generational hot potato they handed you, once you know that's what it is.

If you can acknowledge that your people-pleasing tendencies are likely to originate, at least partly, from messages you received decades ago, then perhaps you can be open to the possibility that they might not be so relevant to the adult life you lead today.

Now think about the messages you got around feelings and your ability to act on what they tell you.

How did your feelings and actions get interrupted?

See if you can tune in to how you felt back then, what you were told about your feelings, what you did with them and how satisfied, or otherwise, you felt with the actions you took. Maybe your feelings weren't welcome, or you didn't understand them, or you didn't realise any action needed to or could be taken. Maybe you always took the same action and got the same disappointing result, or maybe change seemed impossible so you learned to give up trying.

See if you can spot where you still get stuck, if you continue to avoid your feelings or discount your options for acting on them, and you'll know where to put your focus now, as you learn more about authentic feelings and actions in the chapters that follow.

If we don't update the early belief systems that created our inner people-pleasers, we can find ourselves as adults, with jobs and mortgages and families of our own, still trying to earn the approval of our mums and dads – overgrown parent-pleasers still looking for love.

Pleasing Your Parents

We all want to please our parents when we're little. It's natural and for a time we enjoy the praise it earns us and the feeling of belonging it affords. We're not designed to keep pleasing them forever, though. We're designed to outgrow our parents, to separate and start our own families, with our own goals and our own priorities.

Some children never grow out of pleasing their parents. As adults they still seek the approval of their parents, or feel resentful when they don't agree with their life choices. What's worse, they unwittingly create the same dynamic with other authority figures throughout their adult lives, always looking to get it right and please the 'parent' in any given situation. They even create a critical internal parent of their own to comply with in the absence of external authority.

Putting your coat on

There's an idea I use to illustrate this concept when I'm working with these parent-pleasers, and it's about putting your coat on.

Imagine being little. First you put your coat on because your mother (or whoever takes care of you) tells you to. You comply with her because she's the authority and has the power and wisdom to guide you.

Now imagine growing up a bit. Your mother tells you to put your coat on, but this time you don't. There are a couple of times in your development that you'll cycle through this stage naturally, first as a toddler when you start to assert your independence and again as an adolescent when you strike out on your own. At these times you don't put your coat on, precisely *because* your mother told you to. It's about healthy defiance and forming an identity that is different from hers; it's about being separate and becoming an individual.

Now picture yourself as a grown-up. If you have been able to navigate these stages of compliance and defiance successfully, being part of a system and also being your own person, you'll find yourself out the other side and at a place where you can put your coat on *even though* your mother tells you to. Neither pulled to comply with or defy her (or any other authority figure that follows), you are free to be who you are and can make your own decisions. Your choice isn't relative to her approval or disapproval, it stands up on its own. You put your coat on because it's the *appropriate* thing to do in the situation. You don't do it because she tells you to, but you can account for her opinion when weighing up your options. You don't have to rebel against her advice out of principle and you can withstand the weight of her command if what she wants is also right for you.

Defiance is a tricky stage for a developing child to traverse because it goes against our natural urge to fit in and belong to a group. If we're lucky, our parents or caregivers will understand that it's a healthy and essential part of our development and help us along this journey, even when it is challenging for them to manage at times. They will invite our feelings into dialogue, listen to our point of view and validate our experiences even when they disagree. They will offer us support and permission to be different, to go it alone, and to learn through our mistakes without shame. But what if a parent never rebelled themselves because they lacked this permission from their own parents? What if they can't cope with our big feelings or are too afraid of what might happen to us, or them, if we were to leave or change? In that case they might reward us for compliance, punish our defiance or ridicule our difference. They might over-control us to keep us behaving in ways that they feel comfortable with, and we might bear the burden of this as an adult still.

Over-compliance

Do you still put your coat on when an authority figure tells you to?

Think about how you feel when your 'parent', literal or figurative, approves of the choices you make. Maybe you like the feeling you get when they agree with you or support your decisions. What would it feel like if they didn't agree with something you did? Perhaps you'd find it hard to go against the current or see the disapproval on their faces. Perhaps you don't trust your own judgment and rely on theirs. Maybe you accept their point of view so unquestioningly that you don't even notice there could be another way, or a better way for you.

If you were only encouraged to act according to your parents' rules, you might have got stuck in this stage of compliance. Maybe you struggle now to choose a partner, or leave a job, or make other adult life choices, without first consulting some external source of authority, whether that's your actual parents, the oracle of Google or your trusty Magic 8-Ball.

You might feel better if everyone agrees with the way you spend your money or how you raise your children. It might upset you deeply if they criticise your choices or dismiss your opinions. Maybe you've even internalised your parents' messages of right and wrong and act on these by default; you no longer need to consult your parents in real life because they exist inside your head. This obedience can become automatic and it can live on long after your parents have died.

You live out a version of your parents' lives instead of the reality of your own because you don't want to be an outcast but, in reality, the black sheep of a dysfunctional family was often just the one who could see through all the bullshit.

Luke

Luke experienced this pressure to be compliant. He grew up denying his homosexuality to himself and everyone around him, trying to comply with the expectations of his parents and the broader parental messages of his conservative society.

Luke told me he'd been raised deep within the Bible Belt of America, where homosexuality hadn't been an option. He had married a woman and convinced himself that he could live the heterosexual life that was required of him, giving his mother the grandchildren she so desperately wanted. Years of Pacifier pleaser patterns led him into depression and eventually a friend persuaded him to talk to a counsellor.

Luke painfully acknowledged the lie he was living and the love he felt for a male colleague, an admission that could destroy the lives of everyone he cared about.

He kept his secret but separated from his wife and moved to Canada, where he made a new life for himself and eventually found the courage to come out to his closest friends. At last he could be himself, but he still couldn't shake the feeling of shame.

When I met him, he was running a company in the UK and struggling to resolve conflict within the board. One morning he arrived sweaty and breathless, laughing as he told me how he'd had to run all the way from the gym because his trainer had been late as usual. Luke was a confident, successful guy but he balked when I suggested he could tell his trainer that he needed their sessions to run on time.

'But what if he thinks I'm criticising him?' he'd said, horrified.

'That's true,' I'd reflected. 'What if he does feel criticised at first? What if that's part of being true to yourself and making your relationship work better?'

To challenge any form of authority felt shameful to Luke. He was nearly fifty years old and he still let his parents believe that he was straight, even making up relationships to make his situation more believable. A part of him was desperate to stop lying to them but he feared there would be consequences – he'd bring shame on them, lose their approval and with it their love – so he told them what they wanted to hear and kept his distance so that he didn't have to let them down. He did the same at work, telling the board what *they* wanted to hear but creating bigger problems in the process. This became the theme of our work: Luke's willingness to deny his needs or go without, in order to avoid challenging any kind of 'parental' voice.

Distilling an up-to-date parent voice

Like Luke, you might fear that breaking your contract of compliance with your parents might destroy your relationship, even in adult life. If this strikes a chord with you, you might be caught in a stage of over-compliance that isn't healthy. The strict parental voice that you've internalised might shame you indiscriminately, for going against the grain in any area of your life, or failing to live up to the expectations of everyone else.

As adults, we need to review past expectations from a present-day perspective, to reflect on and make new sense of them. People-pleasers often swallow whole the points of view of others, without giving themselves the time and freedom to reflect on their validity. We need to sift out the relevant information from our parents' beliefs (and those of other people in positions of power) and let go of what is no longer useful.

Whether or not Luke decided to address the inauthenticity in his relationship with his parents, he needed help to make more appropriate choices in his everyday relationships. Even if he chose never to confront the original prejudice, he could choose to step out from under its shadow elsewhere in his life and refuse to collect misplaced feelings of shame for challenging authority at work, or at the gym.

Your parents will have had their own reasons for their point of view, as I'm sure Luke's did. You might not be able to engage with your parents in real life to find out about their beginnings, and understand their context, but you might find you can still have a useful conversation with them in your imagination, about why they saw things the way they did.

Putting parents in context

Imagine having a conversation with your parents about the reasons for their rules. What can you discover about their situation and their motivations?

Perhaps you can notice as an adult that there were things going on for them that you didn't understand as a child. Perhaps you can acknowledge that they were anxious and preoccupied, controlling you from a place of fear or ignorance. Whether you are a success or a failure matters less in the eyes of someone you can understand to have been lacking the information or awareness to be a credible judge. Or, if you can circle back and re-hear their words with new compassion, for people doing the best with what they had, does it make a difference to the way you feel about their demands on you now? Perhaps you could even glean some shred of insight from their point of view, a positive intention or a grain of truth that could serve you well, if you could allow yourself to pass up all the other material that was harmful or out of date.

Once you've heard from them, take a moment to hear from yourself, too; how you felt back then and how you feel still in the face of parental input or an authority voice. Think back to the rules you received and ask yourself, what is *your* point of view and how does it compare to theirs? It might be wildly different or it might be just a slight reframe. Perhaps you could even please yourself without upsetting them. One university student I worked with was reassured to learn that her parents were as happy hearing from her once a month as they were to receive the phone calls she felt she should be making every day. 'When we don't hear from you for a bit, we know it's because you're happy and that's all that matters to us,' they told her, much to her surprise and relief.

Unnecessary self-reproach can paralyse us into a fixed and outdated position, stopping us from updating the contracts of our relationships or making any move at all, even when the move we want to make might be one that's well received.

The idea of pleasing yourself is not the same as displeasing others; it isn't antagonistic in that way. The solution to the problem of pressures to please is not to oppose them all outright. We are meant to retain useful parent messages and internalise a helpful parental voice as we grow up. It's the part of us that contains crucial messages of protection and safety and morality. It tells us how to cross a road with caution, or present ourselves appropriately in an interview, or cooperate effectively in society. There's usually good stuff within the parent voice (excepting extreme situations in which a parent was genuinely neglectful or abusive) but without the freedom to also draw on our own wisdom, we won't realise that we can cherry-pick which messages we want to take with us. We must refine the parental voice we received as children to bring it up to date, and it makes sense that the rules of our parents' societies won't apply today in the way they did for them. Measures necessary to protect our parents from reputational risk won't be needed now; in fact they might be actively counter-productive. Unchallenged parental voices are the breeding ground for prejudice and paranoia and it's essential that these be filtered through the generations that follow.

Defiance in the Resistor

If your parent didn't give you the thinking space to reflect on their opinions and update their advice, and you couldn't just swallow them whole in the way that Luke tried to, your only alternative would have been to reject them outright. When we reject a parent's voice entirely, we get to avoid its criticism and control but we can also lose its wisdom. Avoidance of any and all parental voices develops into Resistor patterns. Not safe from the pressure to please, we banish all judgment, throw out the good with the bad and the baby with the bathwater. To escape the parent's verdict, we must also hide from our own honest self-assessment, we sidestep our conscience and dodge its cues to take responsibility and hold ourselves accountable. We lose touch with the part of us that can make wise decisions and keep us safe. We're left with only the 'kid' part of us who knows how *not* to wear his coat when someone tells him to, even when it leaves him exposed to the elements and unpro-tected at times. If you're more of a Resistor you might reject your parents' opinion straight off the bat and do things your own way, even when they have a point. Unwilling to comply but unable to please yourself, you can only defy, as was the case for Fraser.

Fraser

Fraser was only six years old when his parents deposited him at boarding school. His father's parting words, before driving away, were, 'Make us proud now, and don't cry.' It would be a year before he saw his parents or his little sister again. He remembered the tears that would well in his eyes and make it hard to see when he read letters from his mother, telling stories of happy family life without him. 'I couldn't tell anyone how I felt,' he told me, 'you just had to get on with it. If you didn't, you'd be teased or punished. I pretended to myself that they were dead. It made it easier somehow.'

It wasn't the first time his parents had broken his heart. Even before the fateful day that they drove away and left him behind, Fraser remembered feeling the painful sting of rejection.

'I remember asking my mother once, as little boys do when they ask those impossible questions,' he said, smiling, '"If the house was on fire and you could only save me or Daddy, who would you save?"

'My mother paused and said, with consideration, "Well, I'd save both of you of course."

'So I pressed her: "No, silly, you can only save one of us!"

'"Oh," she said, "well in that case I would save your father. We have another child after all."'

Fraser found a way, at that young age, to survive on his own and become, as he saw it, 'self-sufficient at six'. He abandoned all trust in his parents and found some comfort in rebelling against them and what they expected from him. If he didn't matter to them, then he needed them to not matter to him. He began to break the rules and start fights with the other boys, taking pleasure in the exasperated phone calls made to his father by the masters who couldn't control him.

He'd continued to break the rules and was expelled for cheating in his final exams. 'I didn't need to cheat,' he told me. 'I'd done all the revision and we all knew I could have done bloody well but I just wanted to see if I could get away with it.' He had lived a life that was rebellious and self-destructive and now he found himself all alone. Unable to earn his parents' love, he'd built his identity on defying them and all those who followed and tried to tame him.

I was stunned into silence when he recounted that early conversation with his mother.

'You've gone very still,' he said to me tentatively, the corners of his mouth still smiling but with a new melancholy behind his eyes.

For Fraser, seeing the impact his story had on someone else was his first step to reclaiming the feelings he had switched off over the years. Sitting across from the shock he saw on my face, he re-experienced his abandonment through the eyes of a witness, and began to make contact with the rage and the sadness that he had buried. We spent many weeks bringing that imaginary little boy back into the work we were doing, making space for his grief and loss, feeling his way through it instead of defending against it with resistance.

In our sessions Fraser slowly learned how to feel again, to sit with the pain he carried and the losses he'd experienced as a result of his inability to attach to others. His regret at not having children, frozen in fear that he'd do the same to them as his parents had done to him, and the reflexive termination of relationships with women he'd loved, when they had pressured him to commit.

In the safety of the space and with new permission to feel, Fraser began to come to terms with what his Resistor patterns had prevented him from having, what could have been and what had been instead. He recognised the ways he used defiance, detachment and self-destruction as defences against the fear of rejection or cruelty by others. When he left therapy, he was preparing for an extended visit to his sister in New Zealand, excited at the prospect of renewing their relationship and ready to connect.

How did your 'kid' feel?

If you recognise yourself as a Resistor, someone who wants to believe that they don't care what people think, you might want to consider what feelings you defend against. Maybe, like Fraser, you know how it feels to be rejected and you guard against that pain by coating yourself in a protective layer of rebellion and indifference.

Fraser had to hide his feelings as a child but bringing them back into the light became central to his recovery as an adult. Bringing your feelings into your awareness might be important for you too.

Imagine yourself as a child. Ask yourself, how did you feel back then?

See if you can let your early feelings surface but be careful not to dismiss them this time, or brush over what they have to say. They deserve validation; your feelings are sound and there for good reason, even when you don't know what that reason is. Find out what they needed then and commit to helping them get what it is they need now. Don't let your Resistor persuade you again that it's better not to care. You won't need your resistance to protect you, once you know how to please yourself.

Secrets and lies

There is a third kind of parent-pleasing relationship. These are the pleasers who straddle the two positions of compliance and defiance, neither content to follow the rules nor willing to rebel. As children and adolescents, these were the ones who complied in public but defied in private.

They learned to hide the truth and manipulate their parents to get what they wanted. Unable to ask directly for what they needed, they learned to be sneaky and duplicitous in their strategies to hoodwink the people in power, justifying deceit as their only option. Peer pressure in adolescence exacerbated the situation as pulls to please their parents were compounded with new pressures to please their peers.

As grown-ups, unwilling to give in but scared to openly defy, they continue to lie to get what they want, or coerce their parents (and other authority figures) into signing off on their version of events. They are economical with the facts, peddling a whitewashed narrative for the powers that be and running a racket of exaggeration and half-truths. They don't just do it with their external parents either; they can start to hide their truth from themselves and their own internalised parent too, keeping secrets from their conscience. They deny themselves something that they *want* to do because of what they think they *should* do, but end up doing it anyway, silently, passively or rebelliously. These parent-pleasers weren't taught that mistakes are a natural and acceptable part of growth, that they can learn from the consequences and make better choices based on their discoveries. Instead they disown their desires and to the outside world, they look like a Classic, or a Shadow or a Pacifier, whilst on the inside they harbour a secret Resistor.

We all know a parent-pleaser like this because they'll do it to us too. Casting us all into the role of a critical parent figure like their own, they won't want us to be cross so they'll tell us they're running ten minutes late when really it's an hour. They'll hide one problem but create a bigger one in the process. They'll 'forget' they've arranged to meet us when really they've double-booked themselves again. They'll say sorry for letting us down but take no advance action to do things differently next time. If this is you, now's the time to stop. Lying to yourself and others about who you are won't bring you closer to the sense of freedom and unconditional acceptance you crave and it won't reveal the vital information about how helpful or unhelpful your choices really are. It will, however, come loaded with extra feelings of confusion and shame, feelings which were probably already there in abundance for you growing up.

Soraya

Soraya tried to comply with her mum's expectations but wrestled with her own internal saboteur.

As a child of eleven, Soraya had read an article in her mother's copy of *Woman's Own* about a calorie-controlled diet. Soraya knew she was physically bigger than her friends, and certainly bigger than the pictures of the models and the pop stars that filled the pages of her *Smash Hits* magazine.

She copied out the low-calorie foods they suggested and added them to the weekly shopping list. The next weekend, she set about preparing her lunch following the meal plan she had torn out. Her mother scoffed at her plate of crispbreads and cottage cheese: 'I couldn't manage all that and I'm not even supposed to be on this diet!'

Soraya's mother was very petite and, looking back, possibly battling with her own eating disorder. But Soraya didn't know that at the time and all she heard was the message to eat less and that three crispbreads was total gluttony.

The damage that parents do is often unintentional. More often than not it's the little things, the throwaway comments or the roll of the eyes, that tell a child that what they're doing is not OK. I don't doubt that if Soraya's mother had listened to her daughter talking in therapy, she would have been devastated to realise the impact her crispbread comment had made. There were other remarks that Soraya remembered too: the way her mother would cheer her up when she was ill by telling her it was a 'good way to lose a few pounds', or take her shopping as a 'reward' when she dropped a dress size and needed new clothes. Meanwhile, running in the background were all the unspoken messages, like the forkfuls of food left on her mother's plate at mealtimes or the disgusted face she'd pull when she saw somebody overweight on the television. Like most eleven-year-old girls, Soraya wanted to be like her mum, and she began to restrict her calories further, relishing the feeling she got when her stomach gnawed away at itself noisily. The pounds would fall off and she'd reset her goal weight, lower and lower – round, arbitrary numbers, completely detached from logic or science. When she exercised, her mother would praise her for 'working up an appetite', or 'earning' her calories that day.

No matter how disciplined Soraya tried to be, she would inevitably hit a wall and be unable to starve herself any longer. Then she would binge on all the foods that she'd previously made off limits, spending her pocket money on chocolate bars from the corner shop and hiding the wrappers under her bed, until she'd gained back all the weight she'd lost. Food became the enemy and she engaged in an internal battle of wills whenever she ate. She'd set herself stricter and stricter rules, internalising her mother's voice and weaponising it against herself. When the rules became unbearable she'd sabotage herself in an act of defiance, rebelling against her real parent and the punitive parental voice she had internalised, as she gorged on forbidden foods and the double helpings of shame that accompanied them.

This cycle dominated Soraya throughout her twenties as her methods became more extreme. Intense exercise, combined with periods of fasting to please according to her mother's code, followed by periods of binging by a Resistor who'd lost the will. She'd weigh herself several times a day and the digital read-out had the power to transport her to a place of despair or euphoria. She lied to her friends about her behaviour and became snappy and short-tempered with her boyfriend when he confronted her about her mood swings.

Eventually she came to therapy, not about her eating but about her depression. It was many weeks before we even began to talk about her relationship with food and, more importantly, her relationship with her mother.

'So how do you think you'll feel when you hit that number?' I'd asked in relation to her latest target weight.

'Happy!' Soraya answered without hesitation. 'Like I'm finally good enough.'

Soraya's desire to please her mother had set her off on a pattern of self-destructive behaviour that tied her sense of worth to a number on the scales.

In reality, Soraya always *had* been good enough. She eventually came to understand that she had sought to please a mother who was still trapped in extreme messages of self-control and discipline from her own beginnings.

We explored what it would have been like if her mother had responded back then with a message of protection and accept-ance instead, if Soraya could have gone to her with the torn-out pages of the meal plan and heard her mother say: 'You don't need to follow a diet, you don't need to change, I love you exactly as you are. But I am interested in what made you think you needed to look different – could we talk about it?' If she had, Soraya imagined that all of her fears about not being as good as her peers would have come tumbling out and the life that followed could have been one of greater understanding and self-acceptance. As it was, her mother had missed the opportunity to help her daughter understand her feelings of inadequacy. Perhaps she was busy feeling inadequacy of her own. It had been lonely in Soraya's eleven-year-old head and her inner critic had filled the silence.

Magic words

That line of love and validation that Soraya imagined hearing from her mother contained the words that could have set her off on a different path. If we can understand what we've always hoped to hear from our parent, we can understand what it is we need to hear from ourselves now. We can start a new path and be the parent to ourselves that our younger self needed.

Perhaps you can remember a comment that your parent made that hurt you, or that sent you down a path of unhealthy behaviour. Does it still affect you today? Think about the message you needed to hear instead, or what it would take to heal the damage it did.

What were the magic words you needed to hear from your parent?

Perhaps they were words that said you were good enough, or that you were loved and accepted for who you were, or perhaps there was some other repair that could have been made – maybe an admission that they'd got something wrong or were coming from their own place of struggle. You may never hear those healing words from your actual parent. They may never understand their importance or they may not have them to give. It's painful to accept that they won't ever come from the original source, or back at a time when we really needed them.

If we can come to terms with this fact, then we can let go and move on to what can be healing for us now. We can stop pleasing our parents in the blind hope that one day we'll have done enough to hear the words we crave. We can stop seeking new relationships that will fill the gap but that won't actually heal us. We can stop holding ourselves to those outdated conditions of worth that left us feeling insufficient. We can stop pleasing other people and start pleasing ourselves.

Just as we have the power to internalise a negative parent, so can we internalise a positive one, one who can come through for us with those magic words now. Allow yourself to feel angry and grieve if you need to, for what you wish had been. When you've grieved it, let it go. Now give those magic words to yourself, freely and forever. You are good enough. You always were.

Listen for the grain of truth

In all of these cases, Luke, Fraser and Soraya did what they thought was necessary at the time, as children – whether that was to comply, to defy, or to hide. In each case, the child acted relative to the approval of their parent. For us to meaningfully please ourselves as adults, we have to take over the responsibility of approving of ourselves from the parents we've pleased in the past. This comes with the important counter-responsibility for *disapproving* of ourselves when appropriate. That means not kidding ourselves or defending our bad behaviour, or taking advantage of being let off the leash from pleasing others to do whatever we fancy now. To become self-regulating we must be honest about the impact we have on others, not to paralyse us back into pleasing or not displeasing them, but to listen for the grain of truth in what others have to say. This is how we develop our own mature and moral compass, one that can guide us to take others *and* ourselves into account and help us act appropriately as simultaneously considerate and self-pleasing adults.

As adults, we can reflect appropriately on other people's points of view before we make decisions, which is why we don't have to settle for the flippant philosophy of not caring what people think, or taking false pride in being answerable to no one. Pleasing yourself is really about caring enough to listen to the perspective of others, yet not so much that we drown out our own; enough to find an appropriate balance in the moment, one that is up to date and fit for purpose. There may be something important within a message from your parent, or another 'parental' authority, or your own conscience, that you could miss if you're still trying to break away. It's equally important to welcome in your own beliefs, in order to benefit from the wisdom within your own experience that you could disregard if you're forever trying to be the 'good kid'. It's appropriate for you to know better than your parents at some point; everyone outgrows their parents eventually.

On balance, what's appropriate here?

Imagine a scenario in which you're being asked to do something; it could be at work or in your family. Your response can't come from your head alone – the voice of authority that tells you what you *should* do; nor can it come just from your heart – the voice of feelings that tells you what you desire. It has to speak for both. When we're pleasing ourselves, we're always asking: 'On balance, what's important here, what are my options and what is the most appropriate action I could take?'

It might not be a perfect outcome, it might not be exactly as you want it, but it can be the right thing to do under the circumstances and that's the best move you can make. Learning to make decisions that are balanced and appropriate is the cornerstone to pleasing yourself. If you can be yourself and act from a position that is neither compliant, nor defiant, nor a covert combination of the two, you can feel confident that the decision you make will come from a balanced, adult place. And if, on balance, you choose *not* to put your coat on from that adult and appropriate place, it's true that you might not please your parents (or whomever represents authority today). You may not feel understood or accepted, you may not even feel liked. Not being liked is not life-threatening but it is uncomfortable. It's less uncomfortable when you can feel confident that you made the right decision for the right reasons. There's a definition of discipline that I really like, which says that 'discipline is knowing the difference between what you want now and what you want most'. Discipline usually has connotations of rigidity or restriction but here I like to think it comes more from a philosophy of self-control, self-regulation and a means to meaningfully please yourself. You *can* have it exactly the way you want it right now but if it comes at the cost of a relationship, maybe what you want *most* is to find a compromise. Equally, you *can* continue to keep the peace if that's what you want in this moment, but maybe the pain of conflict would be worthwhile if what you want *most* is integrity. Be honest about what you want and account for the consequences of your options to get you closer to the 'right' result.

On being disliked

Learning to be disliked is liberating, for ourselves and for those around us. When others can understand that our intention in being 'dislikeable' is not to defy or dominate them, not to reject or disrespect, but instead to be authentic, clear, available and accountable, then we can rid our relationships of the toxic side effects of people-pleasing. Because when we live our lives according to the opinions of our parents, or anyone else we cast into this position of power in later life, we give up our identity as individuals. Unchecked, the grown-up pleasing child must squat in everyone else's lives, a stateless citizen, beholden to the needs and feelings of others, tiptoeing around their demands without the integrity to secure themselves.

It's also possible that your parent-pleasing actually gets in the way of your adult relationship with your real parent now. Perhaps they'd *like* to meet the real you, to feel released from the responsibility of parenting you in the way they had to when you were younger. Perhaps they were unaware of the signals they were giving you and were responding to their own unconscious beliefs. They might welcome your ability to make your own decisions and take over the controls. When you introduce parts of yourself that you've kept hidden, you give them permission to do the same. Pleasing yourself instead of them can free you both up to create the authenticity that will secure you most meaningfully in the future of your relationship. Because the more of the real you they see and the more of the real them they show you, the greater the potential for genuine connection.

When we can reclaim our feelings, take responsibility for our actions and even learn to be disliked, we can build more rewarding and authentic relationships across all areas of our life. In the next chapter, we'll look at how pleasing yourself can make you a better friend.

Pleasing in Friendships

It took me years to realise that I don't like being in a group. Parties do nothing for me and even group chats on WhatsApp bring me out in a cold sweat. Perhaps it goes with the territory in my line of work, or it's because my original family unit was small and much of our extended family lived in another country, but my preference is for close, one-to-one connections. I can count on one hand the people I really enjoy spending time with, and my inner circle and my outer circle are one and the same. It turns out my rules of friendship are pretty simple: either I'd die for you or I'm not really fussed. Which is not to say I don't like you if you fall into that latter category; I just don't need to be friends with you. Maybe it's because my commitment to my friends is so fervent (there are only so many people you can die for), or maybe it's because I spend my working week connecting to others, but by the weekend I'd much rather spend time with my family than perform in social situations.

Fortunately, my best friend knows this about me and accepts me just as I am. In contrast to me, she loves to throw a party, but her invitation always comes with an extra RSVP option for me, one which says: 'P.S. Don't worry, you don't have to come!' Our idea of quality time together is a mini-break where we barely leave the hotel, ordering room service and binging on reality TV, whilst lounging around in our dressing gowns. At times you'd be forgiven for thinking we'd fallen out as we can spend much of our day independent of one another – she'll use the gym while I take a bath, I'll go for a run while she checks her emails. In reality, it's a friendship full of the permission to please ourselves and it's absolutely priceless.

I have fallen foul of people-pleasing friendships in the past. The rules of friendship are often unclear and, unlike the protocol in romantic relationships or the contract of employment, friendship can set you up for all of the pressures to perform with none of the structure or security. I used to try to put people at ease, crack a joke to break the silence or offer advice when someone was in trouble, but in truth I didn't always want to and at times I've worked myself into positions I didn't mean to apply for. They mistook my friendliness for friendship and the people-pleaser in me didn't want to disappoint.

Friends aren't family

Unlike family, we get to choose our friends. In many ways, this is a good thing: we can opt in to the friendships that we want and choose who we spend our time with. On the other hand, friendships don't come with lifetime guarantees; your sister might always be your sister but you can't say the same about a friend. Friendships must be built and maintained and people-pleasers can have a tendency to try to please their way towards a feeling of security. They might not stop to ask what's a reasonable amount of maintenance or how much pleasing is appropriate. And they can struggle when friends come from different contexts, with different ideas of relationships and a different definition of pleasing.

Friendships, built on an overlap between what we're both looking for, offer a joyous place to meet in the middle. Different friendships will have different degrees of overlap and we might have the casual friend with whom we enjoy going to the gym or watch the football on a Sunday afternoon. Or, if we're lucky, it could be the best friend with whom we share our most intimate thoughts and feelings and enjoy a lifelong relationship of love and support. Whether the overlap is small or significant, as long as it's mutual, all is well.

Unlike family, friends don't have to be forever. The beauty of friendship is its flexibility. It's not family, it's not for life, so we shouldn't feel the same pressures, right? If we find that our overlap reduces in time or our contexts change, or if our friendship is no longer appreciated, we can move on and make new friends.

That is, we could, if our people-pleasing code hadn't conditioned us to panic at the prospect of any relationship ending. We're so used to bypassing our own needs and fixing other people's feelings that we forget we can end friendships when they don't work for us, in order to make space for others that will. We're so busy trying to be liked by someone that we forget to ask ourselves if we even like *them*.

Symbiotic friendships

Symbiotic and co-dependent are terms we often hear in people-pleasing relationships. In nature, symbiosis is the mutually beneficial interdependence between two organisms. In psychology it means an unhealthy reliance on another person to provide us with life-giving resources. Not the food and shelter we would have required in our natural babyhood dependencies, but the emotional scaffolding that we can still seek in adulthood when we haven't yet learned to become our own supply.

Samara

Samara had been friends with Lucy since school, but she came to realise it was a relationship built on her working hard and getting nothing in return.

For as long as she could remember, Samara had been the type of friend to plug gaps and play support roles for her friends. Lucy was a friend from primary school who relied on her for advice and support, and Samara was always happy to help. Lucy used to say that Samara was like the big sister she never had and Samara loved feeling so important to her. She'd take it as a compliment when Lucy copied her haircut and she was honoured when Lucy followed her into a career as a teacher. She even helped get Lucy a job in her school and took pride in showing her the ropes.

Samara appeared to be a Classic people-pleaser. She liked the feeling she got from being there for Lucy. She liked sharing her textbooks and lesson plans, meeting for coffee to read through Lucy's latest assignment and being the first person Lucy would call in a crisis. 'I'm hopeless,' Lucy would say. 'You're so good at this' or 'You're the only one I can talk to.' It felt good and Samara felt needed.

Sometimes we don't see relationships as they are until they change. Samara's boyfriend had been another person that she had to please. She had worked hard to make him happy but he was jealous and possessive and when he accused her of being unfaithful for the hundredth time, she finally ended it. She was devastated when Lucy took his side in the separation.

For twenty years she had been investing in this friendship and she'd assumed that she would be able to call on Lucy's support when she needed it. It wasn't conscious and she hadn't realised that she expected Lucy's loyalty in return, but when it wasn't forthcoming she felt betrayed and turned her attention to other friends.

As Samara withdrew, Lucy became increasingly defensive until eventually their relationship felt more like that of rivals than friends. With Samara no longer a resource to her, Lucy would pick holes in Samara's teaching, outdo her as a parent or embarrass her in front of their mutual friends. When things went wrong for Samara, Lucy seemed to exploit the situation to her own advantage, and Samara felt hurt and confused by the endless competition and one-upmanship. 'I don't get it!' Samara would tell me, exasperated. 'It's like, if I've been to Tenerife, she's been to Elevenerife!'

The movies of our lives

To help Samara understand what was going on, I asked her to imagine her life as a movie, to notice the repeating storylines and characters, and spot the outcomes that felt inevitable.

We all star in the movie of our lives, one that follows a script we're familiar with and delivers us the final scenes we always expect. The friends we meet will play a part in our movie for a while and we'll play a part in theirs. At times, this can be healing. We encounter someone who offers us something we need and we get to take this gift with us, whether they become a lifelong friend or are just passing through.

If they don't become aware of their patterns, a people-pleaser will always have an opening, in their cast, for someone to please. The person they please will already be primed to receive and, without meaning to, both parties will play into past patterns. At these times, the interaction is harmful not healing – it reinforces a familiar and unhealthy pattern of how we expect to relate to others and how we expect them to relate to us.

When Samara brought her feelings into a therapy session, we were able to unpick her complicated relationship with Lucy and look for the movie that had been playing. Samara came to realise that they had been in a symbiotic friendship for years, until she had broken her side of the bargain, and now she was being punished.

'She has to be the best mum or the most popular teacher … or if she can't do that, she has to struggle the most and be the biggest victim. If I'm having a tough time it's like she revels in it. I thought we were supposed to be friends but most of the time she acts in a way that feels like she doesn't even like me. I can't win.'

'I can't win': this idea wasn't new to Samara. We started to consider where else Samara recognised this feeling from, where else she ran the script that she must always be the one to lose. For us to understand her reasons in the present, we had to look at the movie of her early life and understand what role she'd played in the past and what she expected from her supporting cast.

Samara had younger sisters who she had taken care of. She'd done so willingly and enjoyed the praise and appreciation she felt from her mother for being 'so grown up and so kind'. It was what set her apart – her ability to take care of others – and unconsciously she'd grown up with Shadow pleasing patterns, to seek out people who would play the part of 'the needy other' in her adult life. As a child she hadn't stopped to analyse the dynamic in her family, but looking back, she could see that she never felt important for who she was, it was her selflessness and generosity that made her noteworthy. To please her mum, she'd prioritised her sisters' needs. She had deflated herself to inflate them and make her mum happy. The Shadow in her felt good when she bolstered someone else.

Lucy wasn't in the therapy room with us to share her version of events but, knowing her as long as she had, Samara was able to recount something of her history. Lucy had grown up with a father who was rarely at home, and a mother who was permanently distracted. Lucy had been left to find her own path and felt angry that neither one of her parents had guided her or looked after her as they should. When Samara 'mothered' Lucy, as she had done since school, she played the part of someone who would care for Lucy and be a role model, like her own mother should have been. Conversely, Samara allowed Lucy to be another demanding little sister to whom she felt a duty of care.

Symbiotic friendships can seem to co-exist relatively comfortably, until life happens and the parts we play are no longer complementary. What worked OK before we had kids doesn't work any more, what was easy when we worked together doesn't come so easily now, or what felt natural when we lived nearby doesn't fit our lives today. In Samara's case, a friendship that worked when she had no emotional needs of her own and was willing to make all the effort, stopped working when she started to prioritise herself. As one party withdraws the original supply, or changes the terms of the relationship, the other's original feelings of abandonment are triggered and they can lash out in defence. Even though their anger is really about the past, as it was for Lucy, they can act it out against the person they cast into the role today.

Look out for the drama

Perhaps in the example of a friend who always wants to see you, it feels flattering to have their attention for a time, in a way that wasn't true for you growing up. Or perhaps you feel drawn to meet the needs of a demanding friend in the hope that, for once, you'll be appreciated. That's where the drama starts and, without realising it, we recreate the same dynamics that we were used to growing up, always with the hidden hope that this time the outcome might be different. Both friends are in the relationship for their own reasons, chasing each other's affirmation in a way that's meaningful for them and resolves an earlier unmet need. But because of the unconscious way we enter into these friendships, we're more likely to replicate the familiar negative dynamics of the past than to create the new healing experience we might have hoped for. When we repeat our patterns of unconscious behaviour, we do what we've always done and we get what we've always got.

For people-pleasers, who are likely to count among their friends those that have a high need for emotional reassurance or attention, the backlash feels painful. It won't just be the pain we feel in the present; its roots will be in a pain that we have felt before. When humans join to form any group, be it a friendship, a sports club or a team of colleagues, we first recreate an image of our earliest group – our family of origin. It isn't a conscious decision, but we use it to work out what role we'll each play and how we'll interact. It's a smart tool of our human evolution, to predict our friends and foes and adjust ourselves accordingly. Of course when we work out who you are to us, say you remind us of our sister or our father, we might also hold an unconscious hope that you could in fact be the good-enough sister or father, the one that fills in the piece missing from the original relationship. The one that will right the original wrongs.

You might know something of the other person's movie, you might not. Either way, it's important to remember that, in dysfunctional friendships, you aren't really you at all. You have been cast into the role of someone else, a hero sent to save them or a villain from the past. You can't take responsibility for the drama they replay but you can change the way you perform your part when you realise what it replays for you.

Play the trailers

Even if you don't know much about the movie of their life, you can assume they have one.

Think of a friendship that you find challenging and take a moment to run the trailer for their movie in your imagination. What tends to play out in the action?

Perhaps you can spot the familiar characters and storylines in their life. See if you can notice that you are just playing a part, in their scene, on their set, and give yourself permission to walk away if it's not a healthy relationship of mutual respect. Target the relationships where you are welcomed, as the friend you want to be, and let go of those who cast you in a part you don't want to play.

In the spirit of accountability, now run the trailer for your own movie.

See if you can notice the familiar storyline for you in friendships – what role do you typically play? Are you the hero who saves the day, or are you someone who others have to step in and rescue? Notice the role you have cast friends in before and ask yourself who they were to you. Who did they represent? It could be a parent or a sibling, a friend from your past or someone you wish you were more like yourself.

Samara could have told Lucy that she felt betrayed. Perhaps if she had, they could have rebalanced their relationship, or perhaps the truth was that Lucy had never wanted an equal relationship with Samara; she only wanted the one in which Samara would meet her leftover childhood needs and ask for nothing in return. Lucy probably wasn't going to be the right friend for Samara now that Samara had begun to please herself, and sometimes we do have to give up on people, not because *we* don't care but because they don't. When friends treat you like they don't care, you should believe them. Move on. You won't be losing a friend but you might be realising that you never had one in the first place.

Ending friendships

It takes courage to end a friendship, but it's not a failure if it's run its course or brings irreconcilable conflict. It's OK to shed your skin and allow yourself to outgrow a friendship in a way that you can't easily do with family. Some of the hardest friendships to update are the ones that are established early, at a time when it was easier to be accommodating. Friendships formed before the introduction of partners, work and children are likely to need to be updated or ended at some point. It's not healthy or appropriate to hold ourselves to outdated contracts and continue to relate as we did when we had the time and resources to maintain multiple friendships and jam-pack our diaries. It's no coincidence that we tend to make our permanent relationship choices as adults when we have the clearest sense of who we are and what's likely to remain important to us in the future. A shared history within a friendship will only take you so far; there needs to be overlap in the present too.

It doesn't mean it will be easy to end. Friends may have staked more on us than we can deliver. When we shift our position and update our part, they may feel rejected, like Lucy did; it may even be the exact outcome they feared if this was the movie they were re-enacting. We're likely to get pushback. When friends pull out cheap tricks to shame us back into performing for them, we can recognise this as the 'plot twist' that could go either way. The turning point in the movie when we can fall back into character and perform our part, to get a temporary stay of execution and a predictable albeit unhappy outcome. Or we can allow it to reveal that we were re-enacting old drama and use it to make a change. It might leave them with a vacancy in their cast but that's OK. It might shine a light for them on the real source of their unhappiness – dissatisfaction in their relationship, frustration in their parenting role or boredom at work – whatever part we were playing and whichever gap we were plugging. If they want more from us than we want from them, or if we choose not to continue in co-dependency, that isn't wrong. If a friendship doesn't let us be ourselves or doesn't help us grow then it was never really a friendship to begin with.

Lee

Lee didn't come to therapy to talk about his friends, but they became part of a bigger picture about the pressures he felt to please everyone.

He had tried to stay friends with his mates from university for the previous fifteen years. Before they'd all had families of their own it wasn't hard to get together and then there was an easy round of stag parties and weddings to keep them all in touch. The bonds had started to fracture when real life got in the way; there were kids and jobs and responsibilities that meant they couldn't just chuck their mountain bikes in the back of the car and meet up somewhere for the day. Weekends away became few and far between and their attempts to get together with partners and kids were often more effort than they were worth.

One by one, they peeled off and made new friends, with other parents or guys who lived near them now. For Lee that felt OK but for one of the others, it left a huge hole. Jez had always believed that you put your friends first; that's what he'd done, anyway, and he was always coming up with new ideas for things to do or suggestions of nights out. When Lee passed up an offer of beers, Jez would give him a hard time.

'I don't get it,' Lee said to me. 'I thought we were mates but now most of the time he just makes me feel bad. He'll say "bros before hos" if I tell him that I've got plans with my girlfriend, or he takes the piss and asks if I've had my balls chopped off when I'm doing something with her parents.'

Lee was a Classic pleaser and wanted everyone to be happy. He'd try to find a compromise, meet Jez for a quick beer after work and leave in time to read the kids a bedtime story. After a while it wore thin and Lee felt like he was permanently being criticised by Jez for the choices he made. 'When did you get so boring?' Jez would sneer, when Lee got up to leave after the second pint.

Lee came to notice that Jez was the perennially single one of the group, the guy that always wanted to go out on the pull but never wanted to settle down. He gave the impression that his was the high ground, but Lee started to wonder if there wasn't something else going on:

'You know what? I think he's jealous,' he told me. 'I think he wants what we've all got, a nice house and a partner to come home to and kids and the whole family bit. I think that's why he tries to get us all to go back to how we used to be. He can't have it so he doesn't want us to have it either.'

He knew that Jez would never admit it but it helped Lee understand the pressure Jez was putting on him. It also made it easier for him to stop trying to please him, knowing only Jez could make the changes that would make him happy. You can't care about someone else not liking you when they barely like themselves. Lee didn't have to give up any more evenings with his kids to help Jez stay stuck where he was.

Jealousy in friendships

Jealousy and envy often feature in friendships. Jealousy is the feeling we get when we're scared that something will be taken away from us, so we hold on to it tightly, we guard it and we often suffocate it in the process. A jealous friend is one who behaves possessively or who always wants more of your time and more of your attention, perhaps even exclusively. Envy is slightly different but equally a feature of dysfunctional friendships. If you have something that someone else wants, they might envy you. You'll know if they are envious because they'll try to destroy it, whether that's your other friendships or your success or your self-esteem. You can't please someone who envies you and it's important that you put boundaries in place to protect yourself. You can have compassion for their longing for what you have, but you can't give up yours to make them feel better about themselves.

Lucy envied Samara's success and couldn't bring herself to celebrate it, taking satisfaction instead when Samara stumbled. Lee couldn't give up what he had in order to fill a hole for Jez, and he wouldn't have been a 'good' friend if he had. Pacifying Jez wouldn't help resolve the problem Jez had to tackle: the lack of an intimate relationship.

Green-eyed people-pleasers

Take a moment to consider how jealousy and envy feature in your own friendships.

Do you ever feel the urge to guard your friendships, or do you have 'friends' who feel more like rivals?

Perhaps you have a friend who you can recognise is envious or jealous. Remember their reaction to you is more of a reflection of their relationship with themselves than it is a judgment of you.

What if you are the one who feels jealous or envious of your friends? The bad news is that this probably says more about you than it does about them.

Friends who feel envious or jealous are often the people-pleasers who haven't yet learned to please themselves. If we can let go of the idea that affection and attention can only be received from someone else, then we can release ourselves from the need to survive on whatever crumbs of appreciation we are thrown. Insubstantial and inconsistent on their own, these offers of friendship can still be valued and enjoyed for what they are, when we have the means and permission to please ourselves. We don't need to be jealous when there's enough to go around, and giving to ourselves actually makes us more able to receive from others.

Sally

Sally took her sense of worth from her friendship with Preeti, until she realised that the feeling hadn't been mutual.

Sally remembered the dynamics that would play out in friendship groups at school. It was worst among the girls: there were strict friendship policies – who sat where at registration, who was officially your best friend and who you saved a seat for on the bus. 'I guess it was so we all knew where we stood, except that I never actually did. I was terrified that I'd walk into the playground in the morning and the groups would have all changed overnight, like one massive game of musical chairs, and I'd be the last one standing. If my best friend was ever off sick it was awful, I'd feel completely lost all day.' She could laugh at the drama of the schoolgirl politics too. 'I remember, when we were eleven, one of the girls found out that one of the other girls had started her period but she hadn't told her. She took it like a knife through the heart and didn't speak to her for the rest of the term!' We were talking about school days and friendships because Sally had just had the painful experience of being 'dumped' by a friend. At least, that's what it felt like to Sally.

When Preeti moved in next door, Sally thought it was fate. They were both pregnant, both expecting boys and both on their own a lot, with husbands who travelled for work. When their babies were born, they were in and out of each other's houses all day and as the boys got bigger, they'd organise day trips to the seaside and camping weekends with their husbands. When their husbands were away, summer evenings were spent smoking cigarettes over the fence between their houses after they'd put their kids to bed, drinking rosé and putting the world to rights.

When Preeti told her she was moving house, Sally was devastated. As she helped her pack, they made promises to get together as soon as Preeti got settled in the new house. Time passed and there was no date in the diary. The replies to Sally's texts started to dry up and Preeti would make excuses when Sally invited her to bring the kids round for tea.

When Sally saw Preeti in town a few weeks later, she was in a new group of mums pushing pushchairs. Sally waved and ran over to say hi but the reception she got felt frosty and after a few minutes of small talk they went their separate ways, more hollow promises made for a proper catch-up when life wasn't so hectic.

Looking back, Sally could see that she hadn't been as important to Preeti as Preeti had been to her. She had been quickly replaced by new friends, by some other next-door neighbour who was available to drink wine in the back garden and pop round with a pint of milk when she ran out. When Sally was growing up she had experienced a similar situation; after her parents split up she never saw much of her dad. She would stay with him in the summer holidays when she was older but he had other kids by then and she always felt like a cuckoo in the nest. She knew she could be clingy in friendships but that was because she felt there was always someone else waiting in the wings, ready to take her place. She'd work hard to Shadow please the people she admired, to the point where she would actually put them off, or was left with Resistor-like resentment towards them when they didn't feel the same.

Sally could see that she'd cast Preeti in the role of 'best friend' when maybe that wasn't what they were, and she resolved to be more honest with herself in friendships in the future. It was a work in progress, though, and she still couldn't resist popping round with a bottle of wine when she spotted the removals van turning up with her new next-door-neighbour-to-be. She laughed as she told me about it: 'Well at least I can see what I'm doing now, that's progress!'

Best friends forever

Think of your friendships, now and in the past, and notice the ones that work well and the ones that feel more complicated.

What do you want from friendship?

Are you looking for loyalty, fidelity and forever, like Sally?

If so, ask yourself, what are you willing to do to achieve it and is that what *they* want? Are you willing to put in the genuine negotiated effort of attachment or do you hope to simply please your way into their lives?

Your idea of a friend might be a partner-in-crime on wild nights out, or a constant stream of WhatsApp chatter, whereas their idea of friendship might be a wave and a smile in the school playground, or a coffee once a month.

Perhaps you'd prefer a lighter friendship yourself, and you're just looking for someone to share a hobby with. You don't want to commit to being someone's trusted confidante and life coach.

Know that you are entitled to want whatever you want from friendships and be whatever friend you want to be, but be aware that there are no hard-and-fast rules to back up your point of view, only the subjective assumptions you've brought from the past. You don't have to do things their way, but they don't have to do things your way either.

Maybe a 'good' friend is one who matches the investment we want to make and who wants what we want from the friendship. If they don't, it doesn't make them a 'bad' friend but it might mean they're not the right friend for you. Equally, don't let people compare you to the friend they want. If they are measuring you against a job description of their own creation, it's not up to you to meet their strict criteria. You can't have a healthy friendship with someone who is forever judging it against their idea of a *better* friendship, and it's not your responsibility to meet all their friendship needs. Be brave in friendships, be yourself and be the friend you want to be; after all, you might as well be criticised for who you are rather than who you're not.

When we find that there isn't a fit in our friendships, we can move on if we let ourselves. It doesn't make them a traitor if they don't feel the same way about you that you do about them. Maybe their context is different or maybe they need less from friendship. That's not a reflection on you and you can re-audition for someone who better fits the bill. The vacancies in our cast will evolve, as will our availability. If we can accept the fluidity of friendships, we can free ourselves from taking it personally when things inevitably change. Maybe there is an overlap in your lifestyles for a time or maybe your kids get on for now but it doesn't have to last forever. Maybe you enjoy the first flush of honeymoon friendship when you're introduced by a mutual friend, but an evening of connection needn't translate into yet another active friendship for you to dutifully maintain. To make a meaningful friendship, you need to have a vacancy in your cast. If you don't have the need or the capacity for another friend right now, it's OK to smile and say goodbye at the end of the evening. You can be friendly without becoming friends.

There will be friends who transcend context and remain important to you across barriers of time and distance. Friendships where you don't have to work hard to please them or you can both please yourselves. Some of the best friendships we have are the ones that take the least effort, the ones that are still there decades later at the end of the phone or ones where you can pick up exactly where you left off whenever that person passes through town.

Pleasing yourself in friendships doesn't need to be either/or. Either they're happy and you're not, or you're happy and they're not. Good friendships are always both/and.

Good romantic relationships are also built on these same values of mutual acceptance and respect but when we start to feel insecure, our people-pleasing patterns can get in the way of making the intimate connections that we seek.

Pleasing in Relationships

It's typically not what is said but what is *not* said that causes the problems in relationships.

Karina and Eric

Karina and Eric thought their marriage was over when it came to light that Eric had been having an affair. In reality, their relationship had been failing for a long time and the rupture created the opportunity for them to finally tell each other the truth.

They were a 'successful' couple, living the dream in a lovely house, with twin girls and a busy social life. Eric's job in the City brought in enough money for Karina not to work, so she left her career in HR to raise their family, her days marked out by school runs and dog walks. When she discovered that Eric had been having an affair, Karina was left reeling from the exposure of a life she knew nothing about and a husband she barely knew.

When they first arrived at my office, Eric slunk in with his tail between his legs, taking a seat in the farthest corner of the room. He explained that they had come to therapy so that Karina could make a decision about their future. Like a beaten puppy, he kept his head bowed as Karina vented her fury at him.

It wasn't as simple as Eric being the perpetrator and Karina being the injured party. It never is. In situations like theirs, relatively little of the therapy is spent on the catastrophic event itself. Crisis in a relationship, whether it's an affair, or gambling or alcoholism, is like the inevitable plot twist come to pass – the point at which we notice what's been going on behind the scenes and get an opportunity to look at it more closely.

Let the truth set you free

Over the weeks that followed, there came a painful unburdening from both sides about the actions that had precipitated this crisis in their marriage. Eric's job was stressful and he had felt for years that his only purpose was as breadwinner and 'bad cop' parent at weekends, while he watched Karina flit between coffee dates and build close relationships with their children, seemingly unaware of him beyond his pay cheque. Meanwhile, Karina had fostered resentment for years over her loss of career and identity, elbow deep in dirty nappies and the banality of yummy mummies and playdates, while she watched Eric wine and dine his adoring clients and receive awards for his achievements.

Eric's affair was inexcusable but it was also understandable and in a strange way, they both needed it to happen for things to change. As is often the case, it took a crisis to catalyse them into saying what had gone unsaid for so long. In the early sessions, Karina was enraged when she described Eric's infidelity. By the end of our time together, she saw it more matter-of-factly: 'I think the affair was probably the vehicle that took us into a head-on collision but the crash had been coming for a while.'

Both were prisoners to their different people-pleasing patterns. Eric was a Resistor. He had grown up in a strict, patriarchal household, being held to relentless expectations and never feeling good enough. In retaliation, he had developed a persona of risk-taking and bravado. Karina was a Pacifier; set among a family of high achievers, she was dutiful, amenable and unremarkably average in her straight As.

In the beginning, each represented salvation for the other. Eric could be playful and passionate, wooing Karina with his charm and making her feel seen in a way that she hadn't felt before. Karina was a port in a storm for Eric, somewhere he could feel safe and contained for the first time in his life. They had the potential to bring together their differences and use them to support each other to grow into the emotional spaces they'd been denied before. Instead, the opposite happened: life happened, and with it came the stresses of young children and work and family. Instead of pulling together, they pulled apart, retreating to their original positions of Resistor and Pacifier and unable to communicate honestly with each other. Karina wouldn't rock the boat and Eric wouldn't toe the line.

Opposites attract

The thing that first attracts you to someone is often the thing that breaks you up.

That missing piece of your puzzle that someone else represents will draw you to them in the beginning. It could be their free spirit or their spontaneity, their confidence or their stability.

The missing piece of the people-pleaser's puzzle is often the ability to please themselves, and they can be attracted to people who look like they have that quality. If you were tightly controlled as a child, you might be attracted to the person who gives themselves permission to let their hair down. If you had no one to teach you the importance of boundaries, you might be attracted to someone who can assert themselves to achieve their goals. If you were taught to take care of other people, you might be attracted to someone who knows how to take care of themselves. When you can lean into these differences, then you can learn from them and fill in some of the blanks from your childhood, learning new strategies to update your pleasing, or not displeasing, patterns. You can develop your ability to better meet your own needs, and offer your partner new ways to meet theirs in turn. You both become better able to please yourselves and create a successful partnership of intimacy, teamwork and generosity. It's a win-win.

Sometimes you can't lean in, or you don't, and then the qualities that first attracted you start to repel you instead. If, like Karina, you can't relax your conditioning to please, in order to change, you can start to resent those who can. If you don't notice that the way you do things is a result of your own conditioning and not, in fact, the right way or the moral high ground, you might not even notice that you have any blanks to fill.

When opposites start to repel

Karina and Eric were together for a reason and they both had a missing piece of the other's puzzle. Eric put it well when he said, 'Everything we loved about each other in the beginning was still there, it just got buried under a shit-tonne of life.' Karina had brought stability to Eric's life, but under pressure, he resisted its restriction. Eric had brought a permission to be more pleasure-seeking, but Karina wouldn't allow herself to relax.

We tend to fall back on our old ways of doing things when we get buried under a shit-tonne of life. The missing piece that someone symbolised starts to look like an unwelcome intrusion when we're running our original code. What was confidence starts to look like ego, and spontaneity becomes an inability to commit. They're not easy-going any more, they're just lazy. No longer funny, they're just plain rude. Their ability to please themselves threatens the rules you adopted as a child and, even though a part of you is longing to update it, the conditioning wins out. People-pleasers might be drawn to people who please themselves, but they can struggle to step out of their pleasing patterns for long enough to receive the permission they represent.

Of course, it's possible that they do behave in ways that seem selfish at times. They were attracted to a people-pleaser for a reason too – perhaps it was their empathy or their patience – and so this becomes the task for negotiation in the relationship. You both have something to bring to the table but if no discussion is started for fear of creating conflict, or you believe change is impossible, then one or both parties will have no choice but to fall back to their original positions and fortify their original but limited point of view. A Pacifier will defend old pleasing patterns as the only option, if the alternative could be perceived as a wanton disregard for others. A Resistor can reassert their apathy and dig their heels in if they feel forced to obey. This is where the echoes of unresolved parent–child relationships can play out in adult partnerships, with catastrophic effects. The parent-pleasing leftovers come together and re-enact the scenes their younger selves learned to expect.

By the time I see a couple in therapy, each party is typically entrenched back behind their own lines with a yawning chasm stretching out between them, neither one willing to come back to the negotiating table to look for the middle ground, even though it was the potential of this new territory that brought them together in the first place.

Win-win

You don't have to be in therapy to learn how to please yourself in your relationships.

If you're in a relationship right now, ask yourself the question below; or, better still, talk it over with your partner. If you're not in a relationship, reflect on a partnership from the past and see if there's anything you can learn to take with you into the next.

What first attracted you to the other person?

Was it a trait you were missing yourself, or a freedom you wanted to feel? Perhaps you were able to integrate elements of it, to take some permission to be more like them in some ways and better equipped to please yourself. Or, like Eric and Karina, did you fall back on your old people-pleasing code and start to resent them for their difference?

See what happens if you now bring a dose of generosity and goodwill to your understanding of this trait. Maybe you could understand it as a by-product of their early conditioning that needed a little updating, and that's why they were attracted to you. Or maybe you can understand that your own conditioning got in the way of you accepting their permission to relax your own rules. If it's a current relationship, see if you can renegotiate a way forward together that builds on both your strengths and helps you reach a win-win. If you're single now, see if you can pick up the permission you couldn't accept before and take it with you into your next relationship.

Put down the rope

If we don't look for win-win, we can end up lose-lose in a battle of wills that goes nowhere.

In any psychological tug of war, the first step is to put down the rope. That goes for any conflict in which we've dug in and adopted a rigid point of view, whether it's with someone else or within ourselves. We need to get curious about what's going on, to come up and out of the situation, and notice with flexibility what other options we might have. Once we've locked ourselves into a situation of defiance, of 'not putting our coat on because our mother told us to', then we've lost our ability to negotiate as adults, and with it our ability to get our needs met. Being right, or righteous, becomes more important that getting what we need and we waste our energy on resistance.

It takes generosity to put down the rope. When we can be open to the possibility that our partner tugs on the other end not to control us, or defeat us, but to stay upright themselves within their own conditioning, we can volunteer to put down our end of the rope first, to remove the resistance and find out what emerges in its place. If you still don't reach a resolution, it may indeed be time to let go for good, but we can all afford a little goodwill to find out for sure.

Coming to the table with generosity doesn't mean replaying old strategies of people-pleasing. It means willingly switching on to the *genuine* feelings and needs of your partner, rather than meeting only the needs in them that you want to meet, know how to meet or might want met for yourself. These are the limited strategies of the childhood pleaser and not the way to an honest and intimate adult connection. Find out the truth about who they are and what they want and whether you're compatible, rather than trying to turn them into someone you can please, or turning yourself into someone who can please them.

Two sides to every story

There is conflict in every relationship. It could be about money, or family, or work, or sex. The remedy is the same in all of these situations, but let's take the example of sex because it's a common source of conflict for people-pleasers and one that doesn't get much airtime.

In the couples that I meet, typically one party feels that there was more sex in the beginning when the other person was 'making more effort'. Equally and oppositely, the other party feels there was more non-sexual, emotional connection or practical acts of care and communication in the beginning, when the other person was also 'making more effort'. Both parties feel that the other has done something to stop pleasing them and, not surprisingly, both parties feel that their complaint is more legitimate.

This is an example of a situation in which two people become polarised in their positions, pick up the rope and defend themselves against the other's point of view. The same thing happens when we fight over the housework or the children, the extended family or the finances. There may have been a pleasing part of both people in the beginning that worked hard in all these areas for a time, but was replaced by Resistor patterns once pleasing fatigue set in, or one party broke the pleasing contract. When efforts to please aren't appreciated or reciprocated, one or both parties typically become resentful and withdraw their contribution from the shared pot. These are the couples who have stopped giving to each other because they don't feel given unto. Couples who have stopped listening because they don't feel listened to. Couples who may have found themselves in hot water, because of infidelity or deceit or distrust, and only then have the conversation that was needed all along.

Having the conversation that you need won't bring you back to where you started – that's not the point, and the idea isn't to get you both back to those original pleasing patterns – but it can move you towards where you want to be, if you are both willing to dig a bit deeper and better understand both your needs and your partner's.

Radical acceptance

It's not just about knowing what we want, it's also about understanding *why* we want it. If we can come away from the content of our complaint, we can look for the significance we've attached to it and engage in genuine problem-solving. If we can understand *why* it matters to each party then we can stop defending our own singular point of view and use empathy and compassion to accept that our truth is not necessarily *the* truth.

I talk to couples about practising radical acceptance within conflict. I say radical because it communicates that the acceptance needs to be entire and profound. If we can *radically* accept another person's point of view for a moment, then we can look for the grain of truth in it and feel reassured that they will do the same for us. As soon as we volunteer ourselves to accept that there is validity and good intention behind their point of view, our nervous system can drop its fight or flight response and we can get back to thinking rationally, looking for creative solutions and acting collaboratively, now with two grains of truth to go on and the mutual goodwill to compromise.

Who begins the process is neither here nor there, so if you've spotted the tug of war, you can be the one to drop the rope and trust that the process you kick-start will be beneficial to you both. Not because they *tell* you to drop your end, or because your old pleasing patterns insist that you *should*, but because you want to and because you can. You have it to give and you can do so generously.

What I'm going to say next comes with a health warning. I say it on the assumption that you are in an otherwise healthy and functional relationship of mutual love and respect, free from coercion or the abuse of power. In toxic or abusive relationships, pleasing yourself only begins with ending the relationship and empowering yourself to make happy and healthy relationship choices in the future.

If it is a healthy relationship, however, and you are the one who feels you have lost the sexual connection, you can volunteer to re-engage non-sexually, in non-sexual physical affection, proactive emotional attention and practical support, and find out whether this brings back the sexual connection you seek. If you are the one who feels you have lost the emotional connection or the practical support, you can volunteer to re-engage in your sexual relationship and find out whether this brings back the emotional connection and practical help you seek.

Protesting that one need is more valid or important than the other will only entrench the positions, and it will distract you from that all-important piece about significance.

If you want more sex in your relationship, ask yourself, *why* do you want it? Look beneath the initial answers of biology, or libido, or natural feelings of attraction towards your partner, and listen for the deeper messages about worth, desirability, potency or adequacy. What else does sex afford you? Perhaps you also use it to combat feelings of insecurity or jealousy. Maybe there's a task for you here to work on those other needs yourself.

If you want more emotional or practical support in your relationship, *why* do you want it? Again, look beneath the simple argument that your partner should want to connect emotionally, or that chores are shared responsibilities, or that if they cared about you they would help. What else do you get when your partner helps you, or attends to you? Listen for the messages you attach around care, respect, equality or control. Perhaps you have certain emotional needs which, when met through affection or support, help you feel more valued or seen. Maybe there's a task for you here, too.

The same applies to any conflict. If it's about finances, why do you want them to spend less money? Beyond the rational concerns about your budget, perhaps you feel scared when things are out of your control or when someone behaves reck-lessly. If it's about parenting, why do you want them to engage more with the children? Beyond the argument that it's impor-tant for their relationship, perhaps it releases you from the guilt you'd feel if you were to take a break.

Sharing your reasons for *why* you want what you want can help you and your partner work on meeting them together, if you can be brave enough to bring them to the table. Don't get lost in the content of the argument. Stop. Put down the rope and look for the balance. Generally speaking, balance is better and it's what you both came into the relationship to get. It demands vulnerability, however, and that can be scary, so it's important to prepare yourself by understanding what holds you back from having these honest conversations.

Fear can get in the way of risking vulnerability, airing grievances and making intimate and authentic connections. We know that people-pleasers can be deeply afraid of abandonment and this can affect their ability to relax in a relationship, as was the case for Antoni.

Antoni

Antoni came to therapy because of his insecurity. It was getting in the way. He was terrified that his husband was going to leave him and it made him anxious and paranoid. Every time Marc went away for work, Antoni would find himself thinking the worst, that he was having an affair or didn't love him any more. When they had a fight, Antoni would bombard Marc with apologies and peace offerings; when Marc went out for an evening with his friends, Antoni would turn up in the car at the end of the night to bring him home. Antoni looked like a combination of Classic and Pacifier pleasers, showering Marc with gifts and always trying to keep him happy, but his obsession with holding on to him was suffocating. Antoni's attempts to please Marc were loosely veiled efforts to control him and keep him close but they were having the opposite effect.

'The anxiety comes and goes,' he said. 'This week it's been really bad. Marc's been away with some friends. I know he's getting sick of it and that just makes me worry even more. He's stopped answering his phone now and I know it's my own fault – I'm pushing him away. I'm just so scared I'm going to lose him.'

Antoni looked terrified as he spoke, almost childlike.

'Have you ever lost someone before?' I asked.

Antoni was seven years old when his mother suffered a stroke and died. He didn't remember much about her, apart from the banana pancakes she made for him and sitting on the bottom stair while she taught him to tie his shoelaces, but he could remember the night she died as if it was yesterday. He was sitting on a hard, plastic chair in a hospital corridor when he overheard his father talking on the phone: 'It's over, she's gone.' Antoni cried himself to sleep on the car journey home.

Antoni wasn't close to his father; he described him as 'an alpha male' who buried his feelings and raised his son to follow suit. Nobody had been there to help Antoni understand his overwhelming feelings and he was left carrying their full weight with no tools to deal with any of them, dragging them into adulthood and into his relationship with his husband. For Antoni, loss wasn't sad, it was terrifying. It was the end of everything.

Antoni was shocked at first when I suggested that his anxiety might have its roots in what happened to that little boy all those years ago.

'So you're saying that my anxiety might not just be about my husband having an affair,' he said, partly to himself, staring at a picture on the wall behind me. After a long silence, he looked me in the eye. 'It's because I'm worried I'm going to lose someone I love all over again, isn't it?'

Antoni had never talked to anyone about his mother. Not even his husband knew the whole story. He didn't have the resources as an adult to handle his fear of loss and the best he could do was try to prevent it by being pleasing, so that the people he loved wouldn't leave him. Whatever he felt, he looked to his husband to reassure him out of. He needed Marc to tell him everything was OK and that their relationship was secure. Antoni would keep his true feelings to himself and if they ever boiled over he'd beg for Marc's forgiveness. He didn't have the template that it's healthy and normal to *feel* in a relationship. That it's safe. That there is room for rupture and there is the option for repair. Instead he would unknowingly try to hook his husband into soothing him and reassuring him, and he would alienate him in the process. He would deploy every people-pleasing strategy to try to keep him close, and he would end up driving him away.

He left therapy having understood his fear, and he resolved to ask his husband clearly for what he needed – a space to share his true feelings and the two-way permission to risk rupture in their relationship, in a bid to be more authentic and feel more meaningfully secure. It wouldn't be an easy journey but at least he had a road map now.

Spot your self-saboteur

Sometimes the single outcome you fear is the one you bring about yourself through your desperate attempts to avoid it. Antoni was terrified that he would lose Marc, but his efforts to hold on to him were destroying the trust in their relationship.

Let's use the benefit of hindsight to spot how your pleasing patterns might have sabotaged your relationships.

What has been the downfall of your relationships in the past?

See if you can notice how your relationships usually end. Perhaps you are the one who calls time more often than not, or perhaps the other person tends to break up with you. Maybe it's always for the same reason. Maybe you see it coming a mile off or maybe it takes you by surprise. Maybe you stay together for longer than you should, out of duty or a fear of being alone, or you never make it past the first disagreement.

If you can't tolerate the feeling of being disliked, the relationship might fall at the first hurdle. If you find you can't please them, you'll have to get out. You blow it up or find a way to pull the punch and get them to do the rejecting. Or you tighten your grip on your pleasing patterns and impose them on your partner. You suffocate your partner through pleasing them and bring nothing of yourself. Or you expect them to comply with the old messages you received about pleasing other people. Suddenly they find that every Christmas must be spent with in-laws, gift-giving symbolises love, and emails and text messages command an immediate reply. With no room for negotiation or their own identity, their only option is to pull away.

If you can see that there was a self-saboteur involved in the ending of your past relationships, see if you notice what you were afraid of. Were you trying to live up to a view of what makes a 'good' partner or relationship?

'Good' relationships

As a people-pleaser, you might market yourself at the start of a relationship with your best foot forwards, committing to please but doomed to disappoint. In an effort to please (or not displease) a partner, you don't tell them how you really feel. You keep things ticking along by pretending to be who you think they want you to be, or maybe who you wish you were, until one day you can't. They end it when they see your true colours, or you end it when you see them in yourself and fail to be the person you set out to be. As you resolve to try harder or be less demanding next time, you set yourself up anew, to be the person you believe you *should be* rather than the one you are, and so the cycle restarts.

Where did you get your idea of what makes a 'good' partner or a 'good' relationship?

Antoni's father taught him to keep his fear to himself, leaving him the option of avoiding conflict as the only means of feeling safe in high-stakes relationships.

Parents who never disagreed can set up the mistaken belief in their children that any conflict in a relationship is negative or to be avoided. When managed properly, conflict is an essential part of relationships and sparks an important process of negotiation, to contract for a relationship of equals and a partnership that is greater than the sum of its parts.

Maybe your parents did fight, or one wasn't around, or you decided for whatever reason to be nothing like them when it came to your own relationships. Now you might hold yourself to impossible standards and do all the emotional work in your relationships, accepting bad behaviour, or using Resistor patterns to keep people away. Steering away from the dysfunctional relationships you witnessed growing up can cause you to over-correct. Try to point yourself at what you want instead and you'll be heading in the right direction.

Some people-pleasers never discover that they could have had what they wanted if they'd only asked, or if in fact they had stopped trying so hard to have a 'good' relationship and had a real one instead. Perhaps what you wanted was already yours for the taking. Unable to accept that you are desirable, or trust that you are loveable, you unconsciously sabotage relationships with neediness and bring them to the inevitable and disappointing conclusion you always expect. You take away the message that you failed again somehow, you didn't please them or you weren't good enough, and with it you get another reinforcing experience of inadequacy to take forward into the next relationship, plotting it on a course towards another future let-down.

Rustle in the bush

As Antoni's story illustrates, fear is at the root of many people-pleasing behaviours. It's a natural feeling, designed to keep us alive. If our ancestors heard a rustle in the bush, they were supposed to feel afraid – it could be a tiger after all and, if they didn't fear it, and act on their fear, we probably wouldn't be here today. Most of us won't really run the risk of bumping into a hungry predator in daily life, but there are plenty of risks out there that still fire off a fear response. The prickle down your neck as you walk home in the dark, the freeze response as something scuttles across your peripheral vision, the heightening of your senses as the car in front brakes sharply. Feeling fear in dangerous situations is necessary and appropriate.

However, an overly fearful response in relationships is not helpful. Fear is contagious. If our parent or primary carer was overly fearful, the chances are we will be too. On an evolutionary level, we are supposed to transfer our feelings of fear so that the rest of the pack can receive the same warning and get ready to run. We don't all need to see the tiger so long as one of us does and can let the herd know. But what if the rustle in the bush isn't life-and-death and doesn't justify us burying our heads in the sand or running in the opposite direction? What if the fears we caught from our parents were attached to simply saying no, or being alone, or speaking our mind, and we people-please our way out of feeling scared when there's nothing to be afraid of?

Sometimes people-pleasers will have received the opposite message and been taught to ignore their fear altogether. As a child, their sense that something wasn't OK was dismissed or discouraged and, when they were scared, they were told there was nothing wrong, or not to be silly. Trained out of their intuition as a child, they might not trust their feeling of fear as an adult, they might not know which fears to act on and which to disregard, or how to act on either. They might feel a level of anxiety about everything and rely on pleasing patterns to reassure themselves temporarily, or they might not pick up on red flags when they're warranted, staying in dangerous situations or toxic relationships instead of learning how to leave and please themselves.

Protect yourself

When faced with a rustling bush, we can do any number of things to reduce or deflect our fear – we can run away, hide, adapt our behaviour, distract ourselves, hope it will stop, or tell ourselves we're being ridiculous. People-pleasers might do all of these because they lack the ability to validate their feelings and act on them in ways that protect and please themselves. Feeling unable to change the situation, they must modify their own behaviour or flatten the peaks of their terror into perpetual anxiety. When it comes to a rustle in the bush, or fear of conflict in relationships, there are really only two healthy recourses:

Firstly, find out what's really there. Don't assume it's a tiger just because it rustles. Let yourself discover that your fear isn't always founded. Find out what happens if you tell someone how you really feel, or you don't default to old pleasing patterns. If you're feeling insecure because you haven't heard from someone, before you assume the worst, call them. Give yourself the opportunity to find out that it's nothing personal and that they've been dealing with something of their own. Challenging your assumptions and checking out your fantasies will retrain your brain to map out a different possibility for the future, one in which you can stop pleasing and discover you were safe all along.

Secondly, tool up. If you're going to face the danger and not run away, you have to feel equipped to brave the emotional tigers when they do appear. Courage isn't about kidding ourselves that bad things will never happen to us. It's about learning that we have the resources to overcome disaster. You need to know that if you're looking down the barrel of loss, or betrayal or rejection, you have something more to secure you than the fickle affirmations of others. To risk rupture in relationships, you need the protection of self-worth and the resilience to say, 'I will survive'.

Antoni needed to face his fear of loss, rather than try to outrun it by pleasing his husband and denying his vulnerability. He needed to share more, not less, and risk Marc's reaction, in order to find out whether Marc loved him enough to accept his vulnerability too. He could lean on his own self-belief to trust that, if it was only his people-pleasing that kept them together, he could survive the loss of a wrong relationship to look for the one that was right.

If you typically shy away from conflict in your relationship, be brave and investigate; you may have nothing to fear. When you stop people-pleasing you learn that, in the words of Dr. Seuss, 'those who mind don't matter, and those who matter don't mind'. The people who matter already love you for who you are, and it was the ones who weren't important that only valued what you did for them. Conditional acceptance is no acceptance at all and the end of a relationship built on people-pleasing is not the wrong result. Rupture in relationship can be repaired if both parties are willing and if it can't be repaired, the relationship was never yours to begin with.

Pleasing at Work

When I was in my twenties, I took a job at a company where I was part of a department that was measured by our team results. To begin with, I would take great satisfaction in ticking off my to-do list and leaving the office with an empty inbox, clear on my priorities for the following day and ready with suggestions for ways that we could deliver greater value. I was meticulous and organised and would happily volunteer for the actions that would come out of team meetings until, one day, I realised that I was the only one. At this company, there was a curious dynamic whereby if you did your own job well, you got to do everyone else's job too.

So I stopped trying to please everyone but, rather than actively assert myself, I just mirrored the passivity I saw in the Resistors of the team and kept quiet when tasks were being allocated, or skipped the meetings altogether. When no one volunteered, someone would eventually be 'volun-told' but I was creative in my abilities to sidestep the endless actions and earned the nickname 'Teflon Turrell' for my slippery shoulders that could shrug off any extra requests coming my way.

It seemed I knew how to give too many fucks or no fucks at all but I struggled to find a moderate fuck distribution.

I decided to get out of the dysfunctional situation and find a vocation that would feel more rewarding. It turned out to be psychotherapy.

It's not school

Learning how to please yourself is about growing up and becoming self-regulating, whilst still giving enough of a fuck. When you update the rules and supply the missing permissions from your childhood, you learn that being and pleasing yourself is both acceptable and appropriate as an adult. There is no longer an external parent upon whom we must depend, and we can develop an up-to-date internal parent in their place, to guide us, hold us to account, and support us through tough times. Until we go to work, that is.

The traditional work culture can catapult us back to being children. I hear some people-pleasers talk about work as if it were school, grown adults suddenly reduced to the patterns of supplicant children by the overbearing culture of an institution with stuffy dress codes and inflexible hours. Eager to please, they are forced to comply with their bosses and put their coat on for reasons that don't stack up.

That's not to say we shouldn't follow rules at work. There need to be practices and expectations that are professional, and protect workers' rights to do their jobs unencumbered by discrimination or harassment. These aren't rules for rules' sake or for the purpose of having power over others and creating parent–child relationships where they don't belong. Many companies have become more progressive in their approach and understand that flexible working isn't a reward for good behaviour, it's a healthy ingredient of a mutually respectful and collaborative environment. Or that presenteeism doesn't equate to delivery. Or that a zero-absence record isn't proof of superhuman stamina, or dedication to the job.

However, rules that less enlightened employers enforce, to police employees and make them compliant, can crush the morale of a team and tank their productivity. Showing up as a strict authority figure will guarantee you a workforce of naughty children or teacher's pets. Expectations not founded in logic create a power imbalance at work that isn't befitting of an adult workspace and drives employees into a response of insecurity and fear. In this childlike, fight-or-flight space, we can't access our most rational, problem-solving and collaborative selves, and we certainly can't be effective.

Being an adult at work

Being anything other than adult at work is a bad idea. In fact, you can curb your potential for success at work through the efforts you make to secure it. Aiming for the gratitude of your bosses by being agreeable and pleasing erodes your sense of competency and diminishes your credibility. You can end up avoiding criticism and retribution by never deviating from the norm or thinking outside the box. Conversely, a willingness to be disagreeable and assertive can actually make you *more* valued and respected. Disagreeability is part of authenticity and can be helpful, even necessary, in developing productive working relationships. It can allow you to make the impact you want and draw the accolade you deserve. There's a big difference between being indifferent and being comfortable with being different, and having the ability to stand up for what you believe in is vital to job satisfaction.

We shouldn't be scared of rupture within our professional relationships any more than the other situations we have explored. Of course there are the realities of work; we need our jobs and the wrong rupture could have practical consequences that extend beyond those of ending a friendship or breaking up with a partner. But sometimes trying to prevent rupture is the very course that puts your career most at risk.

If we over-comply at work we can also trigger a negative counteraction elsewhere. Maybe we'll cut corners at home or take personal relationships for granted, and justify it by saying, 'Well, I need somewhere I can relax, I can't be perfect all the time.' By creating this distinction between home and work we discount the people we care about, who, in turn become fed up with picking up after us or making do with our conversational leftovers at the end of the day. That's not to say we then need to step up our game and be more pleasing at home as well; instead we need to temper our pleasing tendencies across the board. Being more consistently yourself, imperfect but engaged, across all areas of your life, will help you feel more relaxed and better able to function, both personally and professionally.

To please yourself at work, you need to free yourself from the notion of bringing only your best, most performative (and thus childlike) self to work and start to show up as you are, authentic and self-governing according to your own adult, moral compass. To please yourself, you need to be clear about your motivations so that you can act appropriately, neither over-compliant nor defiant. People-pleasers find it all too easy to do things for the wrong reasons at work and generally suffer the consequences somewhere further down the line, as Chris found out the hard way.

Chris

Chris was a workaholic. He was a nurse manager in a busy department of a general hospital and spent his days making everybody's lives easier. If someone was off sick, he would step in, he'd be the first to volunteer if a colleague needed help and he'd regularly find himself with extra duties, managing the collection for a leaving gift and booking rooms for team meetings. He worked in the evenings, too, logging back on after the kids had gone to bed to email out the minutes from patient reviews, or update care plans for the following day. These things weren't his responsibility but they needed to be done and Chris knew that the department was stretched as it was, so he was happy to help out.

He thought he worked hard because he was helping his nurses to do a good job, but in reality he did it to follow the code of his conditioning. His parents were active members of their church community and they encouraged him to follow suit, to be industrious and to act in service of something greater. As a child he had done this willingly and been praised for his devotion and his diligence, when he volunteered at community fundraisers or led the Sunday School service. He had developed a Shadow form of people-pleasing and got his sense of satisfaction and purpose from championing others, putting his faith in them and helping them to achieve their goals. He never stopped to ask himself whether the cause was truly worthwhile, or whether it was in service of him too. He liked the feeling of being a cog in a wheel that was bigger than him and for fourteen years, that wheel had been the hospital he worked for. Unconsciously, being useful to other people gave him a sense of purpose that made him feel necessary and secure under their wing. He could hide as an individual and enjoy the vicarious praise he felt from helping others on their way.

One morning, he arrived at work and was called into an unscheduled meeting with his senior managers. They announced that the department was facing a restructure and his role had been deemed 'non-essential'. Chris was horrified; he worked harder than anyone else and contributed far beyond the demands of his job description, yet now he was the one facing redundancy. His fragile sense of security, merely on loan from the success he'd facilitated for his colleagues, was whipped away and he was left feeling vulnerable and exposed. He had people-pleased and problem-solved so discreetly and so skilfully that his efforts had gone unnoticed. His employers never saw the hours he put in to help his colleagues do their jobs more effectively, or the systems he created to improve the care received by his patients. When the time came to trim the fat, being helpful backstage didn't justify the headcount, and he was seen as surplus to requirements.

Chris was devastated that he had Shadow pleased his way out of a job. The original code of his upbringing had taught him to support the greater good, but it had failed to teach him how to support himself.

Frogs in hot water

'You know that experiment they do with frogs,' Chris began one day, some weeks later, 'the one where they put a frog in a pot of water and then they slowly increase the temperature? And the frog just sits there? And then they put another frog in a pot of *hot* water and the frog jumps straight out? Well, I think that's what happened to me, I think I was the first frog for fourteen years and I just sat there as the temperature went up and up. I wish I'd been the second frog. I could have saved myself a lot of pain.'

Things shouldn't have ended the way they did but if it wasn't for the rude awakening, Chris may never have been forced to take stock and reset. He may have continued to find ways to acclimatise to the rising temperatures and missed out on important information about the untenability of the situation. Our task in therapy was to help Chris become more like the second frog more often, and to use his instincts and reactions to get him out of hot water quicker.

Chris was so focused on pleasing for the greater good that he had switched off his own feelings entirely and existed only in the realms of the patients and colleagues he worked with, readily treating their discomfort whilst wilfully ignoring his own. Shadow pleasers get satisfaction and security from being part of something important, rather than being important themselves. We needed Chris' own feelings to come back online and for him to reclaim his own importance.

To walk away from pots of hot water in future, he needed to be able to stick a foot in and feel the heat. Only then would he get the feedback he needed to jump out and take his passion and his talents elsewhere.

Sitting in hot water, telling yourself, 'things will get better' or 'somebody's got to do it' or 'nothing worth having ever comes easily' are the classic discounts and workarounds of the people-pleaser, who prefers to pick up the pleasing slack for others than pay attention to their own experience.

Take the temperature of your pot

Let's take a minute to think about the pot of water that you work in.

What's the temperature like?

It could be too hot if it's stressful, or poorly managed, or toxic in some other way.

Now think about the story that you tell yourself about the heat. Perhaps you tell yourself it's only temporary, or that life's like that, or that it's you that's the problem and you always take things too personally. Perhaps you don't like to rock the boat so you Pacifier please your boss or your colleagues. Perhaps you think it's your job to 'take one for the team' and so you Shadow please like Chris? It might be time to loosen your grip on the rules you received so that you can include yourself among the number you support.

If you're a people-pleaser, you may not have noticed that it's the environment that's the problem, not you. It's important to regularly check the temperature of the pot you work in and let yourself take an honest reading of it. If the water is uncomfortable, give yourself the permission to do something about it or get out. There are plenty of nice ponds out there and forcing yourself to stick it out in a scalding pot is the first thing stopping you being somewhere better, somewhere you can feel comfortable and be successful.

Relationships are fifty-fifty

Sometimes in order to say yes to ourselves, we have to say no to someone else. That applies at work as much as anywhere else. Sometimes we have to leave something, or end something, in order to be true to ourselves. Or we have to say no to something that's asked of us and risk disappointing the person who asked. Other people's disappointment, particularly those people we perceive to be in power, feels like torture to a people-pleaser. That's because people-pleasers haven't been told that they are only responsible for fifty per cent, for half of the relationship. We are responsible for *how* we say no, that fifty per cent sits with us. How the other person receives our no is the other fifty per cent, and we can't take responsibility for that. People-pleasers often feel that they should never have a negative impact on anyone else. I would agree that we shouldn't *intend* a negative impact but if one is created as a result of us meeting our own needs, that has to be OK. If someone wants you to do something that you don't want to do, either you're left with the problem or they are. It stands to reason that *the* problem can't always be *your* problem. Setting them up to assume that you are the permanent problem-solver will also incapacitate them and stop them from drawing on their alternative options or their other resources, making them more likely to call on you again next time.

If we don't learn to say no, we will start to foster resentment towards other people for asking. We might convince the world that we're happy to help, or willing to go with the flow, but behind the smokescreen there is often a person feeling bitter and resentful, who harbours rage towards the world and is ready to explode: 'What about me?' / 'I'm always first in the office but you won't let me leave early today?' / 'I meet all of your deadlines and now you say you can't meet mine?' / 'I always say yes to you but now you say no to me?'

Resentment is the felt symptom of unfelt anger. Anger towards others for imposing upon you and anger towards yourself for accepting the imposition. If you notice you feel resentful, you probably need to reset a boundary with the person you resent. You need to define what they can expect of you and what you are realistically willing to give. Pleasers can kid themselves, and everyone around them, that they act out of the goodness of their heart, that they're only too happy to help or have plenty to go around. Unconsciously the pleaser may hope that some of their generosity will be repaid. They feel let down when they realise there was no reciprocal arrangement, no words of appreciation and no award for the 'employee of the month'.

It's going to be impossible for people to respect your boundaries if you don't actually set any, or if you don't communicate them when you do. If you forego your boundaries to avoid conflict, or out of lack of respect for yourself, you can't blame others when they cross the invisible line.

Only do what you are willing to, freely and without strings attached. Doing something begrudgingly in the hope that it will accrue you credit down the line is a hustle; it's a manipulative way of placing someone in your debt and shoring up your future asks.

It might not sit comfortably with you that your pleasing acts aren't entirely selfless. For the sake of clarity, when I use words like 'manipulative' I don't mean it critically. I don't believe that it's a deliberate or malicious tactic to hoodwink someone into meeting your needs. Far from it. It's the unconscious contingency of someone who doesn't trust that they would warrant needs without it. You don't believe you can ask for what you want directly so you scratch their back and hope they'll feel obliged to scratch yours in return. You send a message to get a reply and you help out to feel appreciated, not believing that you would be appreciated or worthy of a reply regardless, and not yet secure in your own sense of self to be OK without it.

The pleasing quid pro quo

On the surface, we please to make other people happy. Underneath, we please to get something in return, as we will see in the case of Rosa.

Rosa

Rosa worked as a bursar in a busy primary school. Every day she would do all the duties with which she was tasked, along with many more. She salved scraped knees, refereed playground squabbles, washed the lost property and drove the netball team to their tournaments. Sometimes her Classic pleaser efforts were noticed. Rarely were they appreciated.

Somehow, Rosa had the knack of doing so much to please the staff and parents that she rubbed everyone up the wrong way. Toes were trodden on when she recategorised the library books or produced a new dishwasher rota for the staff room, and Rosa would often feel hurt by the criticisms of her colleagues. Rosa's solution was to stay later, try harder, be better and please more.

'If only they knew what I *did* and how much I help them, how much the school depends on me. Then maybe they'd say thank you. That's all I want. But instead I get snotty emails from the Head telling me I've upset so-and-so or criticising something I've done.'

As we saw in the chapter on friendships, we can unwittingly get hooked into dynamics with other people that replay old patterns of behaviour. It happens in friendships and relationships and it happens all the more at work, where hierarchies are often in place and invite you back into parent–child relationships. Through our conversations, Rosa came to realise that she had cast her colleagues in the part of her disparaging older sister.

Rosa had been the golden-haired, angelic baby of the family. After a tragic stillbirth, she had arrived to her mother's delight, two years after her older sister. As she grew up, she remained the focus of her mother's affection and felt the force of her sister's jealousy. She tried and failed to earn her sister's love, just as she was doing with her peers now at work. It was a familiar pattern to Rosa as she endeavoured to be pleasing enough to gain a place in the hearts of people whose opinion mattered to her. Yet the harder she tried the more she seemed to push them away and the more they withdrew their affection, the more resentful she became.

Understanding her motivations and letting go of old feelings of inadequacy from her past allowed Rosa to update her behaviour in the present and behave more appropriately at work. From time to time, she still felt the presence of the people-pleaser she'd once been; her spectre still roamed the corridors of the school, volunteering for the odd school trip or unblocking the girls' toilets. But mostly she was able to let work go back to being work, taking on only the tasks that were appropriate and that she was willing to do. She realised how much importance she'd placed on the appreciation of staff and parents in the past, to fill the gap she'd felt in her own self-esteem, and how prickly she could become when it wasn't forthcoming or when they found fault in her work. She put their opinions back into their rightful place, as the valid but not conclusive viewpoints of other adults, no more or less relevant than her own. She stopped coercively imposing her need for validation on her colleagues and took responsibility for validating herself. As often happens, when she stopped hounding them for their approval, she found herself in receipt of their ready acceptance as a result.

No amount of people-pleasing can secure us a place in the esteem of others. Our self-esteem is all that we have to depend upon in the end. Sometimes we people-please to earn the esteem of others but in doing so we often push them away with our desperate need for recognition. Only when Rosa stopped forcing their appreciation could they give it to her voluntarily.

Rosa people-pleased to get something back: she wanted the recognition and acceptance from her colleagues that she'd never felt from her sister. She had to recall this earlier dynamic to understand how she was acting it out now, in ways that weren't appropriate. It's natural; we all recreate our original family in the new groups that we join to some extent. It's not a conscious process, it happens without us noticing, but once we do spot it we can do something about it, and we can get a different result.

Separating past from present

Rosa was able to process past feelings about her sister, to help her update her urge to please in other areas of her present life.

Think about a work situation that you have found difficult in the past and take a moment to scan through the people involved.

Who do they remind you of?

Look out for the behaviours or characteristics that feel familiar to you and see if you can spot who they represent from your past. If you can notice that your manager has the same critical tone as your old teacher or you have a colleague that seems to get away with everything, just like your brother, then you're halfway there to breaking the spell and stepping out of an old pattern from the past.

Perhaps your father was pedantic, or your nemesis at school was an effortless high achiever and you can spot these characters in your workplace conflicts now. If you can recognise that these characters hook you into feeling or behaving in ways that aren't appropriate today, you might be trying to right past wrongs or replay old strategies.

Now that you've spotted it, see if you can separate the past from the present so that you can get back to being your most up-to-date and empowered self, with the permission to resolve differences as an adult and an equal.

You're not helping anyone

Unconsciously bringing unresolved conflicts from our family of origin to the groups you find at work is unlikely to get you the result that you need. It can also stop other people getting the results that *they* might need, as Simone discovered.

Simone

When Simone came to see me, she wasn't sleeping. She had already done some reading around sleep so she knew what to do and had set up a good bedtime routine. However, she'd overlooked one important factor: she would always take a final cursory glance at her emails before she plugged her phone in to charge. Checking her emails, even when there was no cause for concern, was like setting off an overnight security guard in her head, alert to potential danger or intrusion. That's how 'checking' works – it scans for risks and makes us vigilant. It was no wonder her nervous system wasn't ready to rest.

Simone was a freelance designer. She believed the client was always right and she liked to be a 'preferred supplier', always available at the end of the phone and representing excellent value for money. She told herself that replying to an email straight away both demonstrated her commitment and cleared the decks for the following day. Beneath the practicalities lay a more interesting dynamic around pleasing. By pleasing her clients in that way, replying to them late at night and being at their beck and call, she was effectively training them to expect it. John was one such client, who had been trained to expect an instant reply. He demanded a lot from Simone and would complain about the costs or the time things took, regularly reminding Simone that he had 'mouths to feed as well, you know'.

We'd worked hard on Simone valuing herself more, at home and at work. She told me she hadn't put her prices up for five years and stood to make a loss on the next job John had asked her to do.

'I just feel bad!' she said. 'What if I put my prices up and he can't afford it?'

'That certainly sounds like a problem,' I said. 'But it doesn't sound like your problem.'

Propping up the wrong relationships

Rationally, Simone knew that you have to take the rough with the smooth in business. In reality though, she tended to take on the rough and dish out the smooth. She preferred to weather her increasing costs and freeze her prices to keep clients happy, but she was losing a lot of money to keep others afloat. It happens to people-pleasers a lot. They take on the pain, to prevent someone else from feeling it. But letting someone fail is not necessarily the wrong thing to do. It can be necessary for someone to fail in order to reset their expectations or change whatever it is they're doing that's not working. If you take the scaffolding down and the building crumbles, it doesn't mean you failed to support it sufficiently, it means the building wasn't sound. If you say no and someone is disappointed or something fails, it doesn't mean you should have said yes.

It happens in families, too – maybe your mother had to please her mother, so you now have to please your mother, and your child will have to please you. Everyone is pleasing to protect each other from the truth, keeping up the conspiracy and propping up the rubble. Except without an awareness of the reality we mask with our people-pleasing, how can we ever make progress or improve anything?

Eventually Simone resolved to stop making excuses and quote for what the work was worth. John decided to take his business elsewhere, as Simone had predicted. There was one invoice outstanding for quite a substantial amount from him and I asked her what she planned to do.

'Yes ...' she said. 'I think I'll just write that one off to give us a clean break.'

'I guess you could choose to do that,' I replied, 'but it sounds like quite an expensive way to say "no hard feelings".'

Simone laughed and recognised that, even at the end of the relationship, she was willing to lose money to avoid conflict. It's what happened at home as well – she was a people-pleaser there, too, and would regularly take the path of least resistance with her husband and her children. But just because we'd accept some bad behaviour from our teenagers, or an occasional bad mood from our partner, it doesn't mean we have to accept it at work. Work is not personal and, if colleagues behave badly, we don't have to maintain the relationship beyond professional courtesy. If customers don't pay, we don't have to write off the debt. If our boss sends us messages late at night, we don't have to reply.

Simone's fear was that if she 'lost' this client she'd feel the impact on her bottom line. But she was already losing money working with him, not to mention the sleep and the opportunity to work with another, better client. Never ignore the opportunity cost of giving badly behaved people your precious time and energy.

Training bad behaviour

Simone was a good example of a Pacifier who had fallen into a trap of inadvertently training people to behave badly, by allowing their bad behaviour to go unchallenged. She also performed as a Shadow, picking up the slack, often at great cost, to shield others from a reality which, although uncomfortable, could be necessary information for them to be successful in the long run. As is often the case with people-pleasing, we protect others from a reality they fear but that is also likely to be one they need to face. If you are a people-pleaser at work, stop doing more than you're willing to do and accept that it might have an impact on someone else. Leave them with that uncomfortable task of resolving their own needs, independent of you. Don't tiptoe around a relationship for fear it won't bear your weight. Stop plugging their gap with your sacrifice. The taste might be bitter to start with but, in the right relationships, the shift can be positive – and not just for the people-pleaser.

If we don't learn to say no, or if we stay in a work environment where we can only be accepted in compliance, our silent defiance can mutate into passivity and our only option will be to act it out in secret and develop Resistor patterns. We might seek to coerce others like Rosa, or martyr ourselves like Chris, or lie awake like Simone, wishing we didn't care but still feeling the pressure to please nonetheless.

Passivity in people-pleasing

To be 'passive' means to give up our agency in the face of conflict, submit to the inevitability of a situation or seethe in secret. If someone asks you to do something and you say yes, but later you tell them you didn't get round to it, this could be an unconscious, passive part of you resisting their demand by letting time pass, getting busy with other things, or simply 'forgetting'. You didn't actively defy them because that would go against your people-pleasing principles and yet it 'just turned out that way'. It's a last-ditch attempt to have some say in a world where none has been afforded to you. People-pleasers might not look passive, in fact they might look more active than most. They look busy helping everybody but, because they are unable to take responsibility for their choices or prioritise accountably, they can end up letting one person down in order to please another.

We may want to appease people so we'll cram more into our schedules than we can realistically achieve but end up late for every meeting. We might say yes to actions but need a colleague to bail us out when we can't keep up. We'll skim the email but miss the vital information. We don't want to say no but we don't have the capacity to *mean* yes so we fall short and feel like we've failed. The objective reality of the over-promising pleaser is a chronic under-deliverer. On the receiving end is someone saddled with the fallout from optimistic timings or over-ambitious plans. When we inevitably let them down we can only hope that it's our intentions by which we're measured and not our actions or our output.

Or we can become manipulative, like Rosa, and make pleasing deposits in our 'relationship accounts' in the hope that we'll be entitled to make a withdrawal when we need to. We set people up to be there for us in the future by accruing pleasing credit in advance. For example, the employee who bends over backwards to accommodate the demands of the job, just so that they can demand something in return, whether that's a last-minute holiday request, flexible working or a pay rise.

Sometimes we might find ourselves acting defiantly at work, if we lack the permission to be assertive and autonomous. We silently resist the parent figure that we work for, maybe in the way we did with our real parent. We challenge every request out of hand, or behave obstructively to express our discontent. When we're asked to do something by a 'parent' figure at work, we won't say no outright but we'll do it to our own timescale, or to the standard that we deem sufficient, or in a way that we believe is better, even though it's not what was asked.

Recognising your own passivity

Do you recognise yourself in any of these passive behaviours?

Perhaps you've over-promised at work to try to please someone, or to avoid displeasing them. Or perhaps you procrastinate to assert some sense of control in the face of dominating pressures to comply from the present *or* the past.

If you do, take heart from the fact that the passive behaviour is more likely to elicit a negative reaction than the truth it tries to hide. The passivity, and its consequence, is the part that will let people down or communicate disrespect. That's the part that will get the people-pleaser rejected and fulfil their lifelong prophecy that nothing they ever do is good enough.

If you recognise yourself as a people-pleaser at work, give yourself this permission: do it, or don't do it, but don't resist. Work extra hours if that's something you're willing to do, in isolation of any other expectations you have. Ask for what you need, independent of any pleasing groundwork you've laid, and be prepared for conflict and compromise. Tolerating the conflict, in order to be authentic and get a real result that feels meaningful, is the art of being disliked for all the right reasons and is the way towards pleasing yourself.

Please Yourself

It can feel tough to be disliked at work but at least we can fall back on our professional position to help us take things less personally. It can be harder to tolerate being disliked when it's your own children who dislike you.

Pleasing as a Parent Yourself

People-pleasing in parenthood starts before a baby is even born. As we embark upon becoming a parent, we can find we have entered into a new arena of judgment that we haven't encountered before.

The pressure to people-please during pregnancy takes place on a very public stage. In the later stages of my first pregnancy, I would walk down the road and perfect strangers would gravitate towards me, arms outstretched, ready to stroke my baby bump and offer up their evaluation of whether it was 'neat' or 'huge' or 'all round the back'. I listened to their grizzly stories of childbirth and nodded as they dispensed their advice for labour, too tired by then to put up a fight or protect what remained of my privacy.

I chose to find out the sex of my baby, as my mother had with me, and I loved being able to imagine the person I was going to meet. It quickly became clear that this was not the norm for everyone, however, and more often than not, my choice to find out was met with a look of pity and disappointment. Apparently, I was ruining the surprise. I, on the other hand, was of the opinion that ejecting a baby from my nether regions and being responsible for its survival thereafter would be sufficiently surprising. On the day of the twenty-week scan, I was intercepted by a colleague as I was leaving the office:

'So? Are you going to find out what you're having?' she asked me, pointedly.

I already knew what would come next.

'Wow! Really?' she said, looking completely baffled when I answered her. 'I just can't imagine wanting to find out! That magical moment when you're in labour and you need that final push to meet your beautiful baby, and find out if it's a boy or a girl ... it's nature's most wonderful surprise! I just wouldn't want *anyone* to miss out on that moment.'

She stopped me as I walked past her desk the following day.

'*Sooooo*, what is it?'

On that occasion, the potential of not being liked was worth the smug satisfaction I felt as I replied, 'Oh, don't worry, I know how much you like the surprise so I've decided I'm just not going to tell YOU.'

Failing to please other parents

Feeling disliked as a parent by other parents is awful: feeling that you aren't up to the job or that you're making terrible choices that will somehow disadvantage your newborn for life. And there are so many choices to make, all bestowed with monumental significance and governed by self-appointed judges, eager to proclaim their individual experiences as the rule of the land and 'best for baby'. Whether to breastfeed or not (you must), go back to work or not (you must not), feed them shop-bought puree or not (only in an absolute emergency, if your freezer has defrosted and your ice-cube trays of 'Cheeky Cherub's Fruity Couscous' have to be fed to the dog – but even then, it only takes ten minutes to knock up some easy-peasy-cheesy scones, so really there's no excuse, is there?). It's easy to feel like you're failing when you have a baby.

Jai

Jai was a new mum. She came to therapy with a diagnosis of postnatal depression when her baby was three months old. Aalia's birth had been traumatic for both of them and Jai was suffering from intrusive thoughts and flashbacks.

Aalia would join us for our sessions, usually sound asleep in a car seat which Jai would rock gently with her foot. She watched her baby thoughtfully as she spoke. 'The other day I was in the shower,' she told me, 'and I caught myself wondering if it wouldn't just be better for everyone if I'd died in the operating theatre. My husband could have given Aalia a good life without me fucking everything up ... and she wouldn't know any different, would she, so it's not like she'd miss me if I wasn't here.'

She went on to tell me that a few days before, Jai's husband had taken their daughter out in the pushchair while she tried to catch up on some sleep. Aalia had woken up from her nap too soon and began to cry as her tired body fought to get back to sleep. A passing lady had stopped to comment to her companion, in a loud and critical voice, 'That poor little lamb! Honestly, *where* is the mother?'

Her husband was incredulous as he recounted the busybody's comment but it was the final straw for Jai, who already felt like she was failing at being a mother. Her husband tried to persuade her that it wasn't worth worrying about but, having not slept for months, and having tried her hardest to work out how to take care of this new little human, Jai found herself having dark thoughts. She told her husband and made an emergency appointment with her GP.

Depression is a risk for the Resistor at times like these, when their skin doesn't feel as thick as usual and they can't reject the pressures to please as they ordinarily might. In the end, Jai couldn't tolerate being judged any longer, by the health visitors who came every other day, by the rosy-glowed mothers breastfeeding with ease beside her, by her mother-in-law whose children had all slept through the night from six weeks (apparently). She felt lost in a sea of disapproval and as though nothing she did would ever be good enough. Jai had started to withdraw from the world and from Aalia, handing her baby to visitors so that she could take her time making the tea in the kitchen, and finding ways to be alone whenever she could.

Jai told me that before she'd become a parent, it had never bothered her when people didn't agree with her choices. As head of a customer service department, she was used to receiving criticism and making unpopular decisions, and she'd always felt like the odd one out in her family. She survived as a Resistor and feeling judged was nothing new but, she came to realise, the feeling of being disliked for who she was as a parent was something else entirely. Like every new parent, she was making it up as she went along, yet with generations of past parents and 'expert' opinions suddenly crawling out of the woodwork, and without the courage of her own convictions, she felt crushed by their judgment and up against an overwhelming pressure to get it 'right'. Defending herself against the constant scrutiny she came under for her choices as a mother was undermining her confidence in her ability to take care of her baby. Now that she couldn't simply *not* care, her Resistor patterns were redundant and left her undefended in the line of fire. The comment from the woman in the street had, in that moment, represented all of these criticisms, all of the ways that Jai was failing to get it right, for Aalia and for everyone else.

As she rocked the car seat with her foot, she said, 'Maybe that woman was right – I probably should have been there. I'm her mother, aren't I? I'm supposed to be there. I mean, look, I'm not even doing this right, am I? If I was a good mother I would be cuddling her now but she's stuck in a car seat on the floor, poor thing. I just feel sorry for her having me as a mum.'

I looked at Aalia, snuffling peacefully, and I looked at Jai, tuned in to her tiny baby, rocking her gently and doing what she could for her in that moment, giving her what she had to offer and opening up to me bravely in the hope that things could get better. Aalia stirred and Jai shushed her softly. We would come to learn together that somewhere in Jai's past was someone who had never given her the attention she was giving Aalia in that moment.

'You know what? I reckon that's all she needs right now,' I said, 'and what you're already doing is absolutely good enough. *You* are good enough.'

The thin skin of parenthood

Even if you're not someone who typically feels the pressure to please others, you can still find yourself blindsided by the exposure of pregnancy and early parenthood. With your growing belly, physically you are more visible than ever, and you'll draw more attention than you might be used to. Or maybe, like Jai, you're someone who can usually weather people's opinions but when they cast judgment on your baby, you revert to feeling the full force of their assault.

If ever there was a time to take blanket permission to just please yourself, it's when you're pregnant or have a tiny baby. Most new parents are just doing what they can to get through the night and the opinion of other people will usually have more to do with their own narrative than it does with you. Don't mislead them into thinking they're entitled to comment, or that they need to know. You have a baby now and you were a baby once; treat yourselves with the compassion and protection that you both deserve.

Trauma and the people-pleaser

Even if you have an 'easy' pregnancy and a birth without complications, you will still have an enormous amount of adjusting to do as you get used to life as a new parent with all of the uncertainties and first-time experiences this throws at you.

If, as for many women, pregnancy isn't plain sailing or you leave hospital feeling like you've been run over – with a tiny creature to take care of, instead of the round-the-clock care and convalescence by the sea that might seem more befitting of your trauma – then you will certainly have a long journey of recovery ahead.

The reality is you probably won't get to make that journey of recovery, because of the aforementioned creature that you're trying to keep alive, and any other children you might have, and the partner, and all the life obligations that require you to keep the show on the road.

The reality is that a people-pleaser often doesn't get to make any journey of recovery because they are rarely their own priority, whether they have had a baby or not. It applies if you've ever had a miscarriage, or an attempt at IVF, or a pregnancy that just never was. It applies if you've partnered anyone through an experience like this. It applies if you were ever that baby yourself, balanced on the lap of someone reeling from the shock of your arrival. We all hold trauma somewhere and it's never too late to go back and take a step on that journey of recovery.

Re-recovery

Take a moment to picture yourself as you were back then, somewhere in a time that felt painful or traumatic.

Do you know what you needed?

If you can connect with your old feelings and hear
from them what you needed at the time, make a
promise to yourself that you will honour that journey
of recovery now. Prioritise your self-care, front-load your
self-compassion, give yourself the time and space to rest
and process your experience and let its meaning settle
with you.

Perhaps you hold feelings of regret or disappointment,
or anger or fear. These are all normal responses to
abnormal situations, these are the ingredients of grief
and if we can allow ourselves to stop and sit with them for
a time, the hope is that they will pass and we can continue
on our way, not healed necessarily but a little less broken,
and with new meaning that can help us to move forwards.

Pleasing your children

Pleasing a small child can be glorious. The uncontrolled giggling; the clammy palms pressed against your cheeks as they plant impassioned kisses on your face; their sweet, warm breath on your face as they sleep soundly next to you in the early light; the feeling that you are the only thing in the world that means anything to them in that moment. In contrast, feeling rejected by a child can be heartbreaking, whether it's the toddler who howls when you give them the wrong colour cup, or the teenager who hates you for the way that you breathe. But being willing to be disliked by our children is one of the greatest gifts we can give them. We have an opportunity to offer them a safe test bed for their experiments, to give them a genuine reaction and to provide valuable data on how they impact others, within an unconditionally loving environment. As parents we need to free our children from being pleasing to us and we need to free ourselves up to displease them.

Of course they may not thank you for this. It might feel nicer for them, and you too perhaps, if you reacted positively to their every move, bent to their every whim and looked the other way when they behaved antisocially. They might temporarily like you better for this. We often hear a parent declare with delight, 'We're more like best friends!' – meaning, my child likes me, they choose to hang out with me and they want me around. However, there's a design flaw in procreation. Children are designed to outgrow their parents but parents aren't designed to outgrow their children. Having a child who always wants you around is one way to circumvent this dilemma. But on what terms? That you subscribe to the view that your child can do no wrong, that it's always someone else's fault and they have the right to do exactly as they please?

It's vital to ground kids in self-esteem, teaching them through your actions of love and validation that they are worthy of their own. But it's deeply irresponsible to prioritise *your* need to be liked as a parent over *their* need for safety and security. If you don't teach your children that actions have consequences, the world certainly will. And the world will be a much less compassionate instructor.

When parents split up

When parents separate, the stakes can feel even higher. Even when the writing is on the wall and the relationship is over, parents can understandably cling to the hope that they can stay together for their children and save them from a painful path of grief and loss. One client I worked with was wracked with guilt for finally kicking her husband out after years of aggressive behaviour. Even after he'd left, he continued to behave badly; he was jealous and paranoid and would stalk her to see if she was with another man, or break into their house in the middle of the night. He didn't see the kids or pay any maintenance, running up debt on credit cards in their joint names until eventually the bailiffs came to the house to collect. When we talked about why she wasn't divorcing him to settle matters once and for all, she told me she was terrified that her children would grow up to hate her. In her worst fantasies her husband would kill himself and the children would blame her for it. She hoped, somewhat naively, that she could tolerate his bad behaviour and give up on her own happiness to avoid upsetting the children more than they already were. Her friends had tried to reassure her with empty platitudes, telling her the children would understand eventually and they'd always love her, no matter what. It wasn't working and I had to take a different tack, one that was harder to hear but more authentic: 'And what if they did blame you?' I asked. 'Would that be a reason to keep you all stuck in this toxic situation? It's not up to them to know what's right – after all, they're just kids, maybe they need their mum to know that for them.'

Don't ask your kids to know what's best for them. As much as they might protest, kids need you to know better. They need to push against you until they hit something solid that they can be secured by. Without a wall against which they can rail and rest, they have to keep looking for the limits, unable to do the rich development that can only happen once they are safely held in something bigger, older and wiser than them. They need clear boundaries, even if they don't always like you for imposing them.

Say what you mean

Maybe you say yes because you don't want the drama. That's on you and the chances are you're training them to use drama as a means to getting what they want. Maybe the answer was no but you don't want them to dislike you, so you just ignore the behaviour for now or call it 'cheeky' to make it more palatable, or you say yes under duress in the moment but snap at them for it later down the line.

Maybe you say no because you're scared of losing control or you worry that if you give an inch, they'll take a mile, you'll set a precedent or make a rod for your own back. Sayings such as these make us believe there is a 'right' way of doing things.

There isn't a right way and none of this stuff works perfectly, but that's OK because it's supposed to be a process of trial and error and it will be different for everyone. If there was only one right way, we'd all be doing it by now.

If you don't actually mean no and you just think you *ought* to say no, your rationale won't stand up under their cross-examination. You will crack under pressure, or your messages will become inconsistent and trigger a renewed round of testing. If the answer is genuinely and appropriately no, it will be easier to uphold.

If your child asks for ice-cream and you say no for good reason, but roll your eyes when they smile at you and help themselves from the freezer, be honest with yourself about what you're teaching them. Teaching your kids to mollify an authority or manipulate a system in order to get what they want is going to cause them problems in later life and they need you to take responsibility for that fact. They cannot do it for themselves. I know it's not easy to hold the line sometimes, and I'm reminded of a conversation I had with my daughter, then aged four, in which she wanted us to go somewhere but hadn't been listening to me up to that point. 'Well,' I began, 'it's going to depend on a certain person's behaviour from now on.' She thought for a moment before she responded, 'You look fabulous.'

Hindsight, 'mid-sight' and foresight

If you've trained your kids into ignoring what you say, you can retrain them by sticking to your guns, but first you'll need to spot where your boundaries are weak. Generally speaking, we can start this process of behaviour change by first noticing with hindsight what we *did* – 'I said yes to something this morning when really I meant no.' Then we can notice with mid-sight what we're *doing* right now – 'I'm saying yes again when I should be saying no.' Then we get to notice with foresight, ahead of the drama, what we *will do* – 'This is one of those situations where I will typically feel guilty for having to work, so I'll compensate by saying yes to them playing computer games, even though it's really time for bed ... OK, now I know that, I can think through my other options in advance and work out what's most appropriate.' That clear, consistent boundary is what your children are actually looking for when they test you. Let them get there quicker. Some of my clients are the grown-up children of people-pleasing parents, still looking for that something solid, decades later.

The damage of indifference

The same principle applies with teenagers, although this round of rebellion can look more dangerous. Neurologically, teenagers are a bit like giant toddlers, going through a similarly drastic period of brain development but with the means to get themselves into stickier situations and the consequences to match. Raising adolescents can be challenging, and there are undoubtedly times of conflict and difficulty for both parent and child. Sometimes parents can unwittingly seek to right their own childhood wrongs in the ways they parent their own child and, perhaps for fear of over-controlling, people-pleasing parents can end up under-controlling instead. In the lack of boundaries that results, children can perceive a lack of care and this inferred indifference is what does the damage. Rules for rules' sake are as damaging at this time as any other, but the teenage brain needs guidance, it's not wired up yet.

Yasmin

Yasmin wanted her mum to care enough to put in the boundaries she needed to protect her, she just didn't know it.

Yasmin came to see me when she was seventeen and her mum was at her wits' end. Yasmin was regularly skipping classes and was threatening to drop out of college altogether. Her mum told me that she loved Yasmin but didn't know how to help her; she had tried everything and was now at the end of her tether.

Yasmin's father had been a violent man and, after her parents had eventually separated, she'd shared a bedroom with her mother, in a tiny flat above a shop. They did everything together and sounded more like friends than mother and daughter. Everything had changed when her mum met her step-dad. Suddenly, Yasmin had her own bedroom in a new house and before long, her baby step-sister arrived.

Time passed and Yasmin began to withdraw. She told me she remembered feeling like the outsider in her family. When she was thirteen she would have 'temper tantrums', according to her mother, and storm upstairs to her bedroom. Her step-dad would go to follow her and bring her back down but her mum would tell him to leave her be and let her cool off. So she would stay in her bedroom, listening to the three of them chatting downstairs at the table, hearing the laughs and the clink of the cutlery at their family dinnertime without her. Nobody ever came to see if she was OK and eventually she took to keeping stashes of food in her bedroom so that she barely had to come downstairs at all.

This became the way of things, Yasmin would defy her parents in some way and her mother would shake her head and say, 'I just don't know what to do with you, Yasmin, I'm at a loss.' At night Yasmin would lie in her bed and cry herself to sleep, hoping that her mum might hear and come to find out what was wrong. The anorexia that developed wasn't a conscious choice, but it was a way for Yasmin to make her pain visible; she got smaller and smaller and her mother would look at her quizzically but when Yasmin told her to stop staring, that's exactly what she did. She never asked her what was wrong and she never tried to make her eat.

When Yasmin took a waitressing job at a local hotel it was partly for the substitute family it provided. The manager was warm and affectionate and would lay her a place at the staff table after the dinner service was over. These were some of Yasmin's happiest times – she had found a set of replacement parents and siblings who were interested in her and gave her their attention. It also made the contrast to home even starker and Yasmin never wanted to go back at the end of a shift.

Some of the girls at the hotel shared a flat and they invited her to sleep on their sofa whenever she wanted. Eventually, the only time Yasmin would go home was to pick up more of her stuff or to see her younger sister. Her mother would hover in the kitchen making polite conversation while Yasmin helped her sister with her homework, but the discussion never went any deeper.

Her mother joined us towards the end of our sessions together and Yasmin was able to tell her some of what she'd told me. She was devastated to hear that Yasmin thought she didn't care. She told us that she hadn't wanted to upset Yasmin or make things worse and that's why she'd never pushed it. She thought she was doing the right thing by just letting Yasmin be; she'd told herself it was just a teenage phase and that Yasmin would come round by herself. Time and time again she'd thought about going to the hotel to ask her to come home but she'd stopped herself because she thought it would start another fight. The truth was, her mother was scared of conflict and always had been, even with her own daughter. It was how she'd been brought up and it had translated into the way she parented.

Yasmin had needed to know that her mother cared about her enough to set boundaries and keep her safe. Her mother was a Pacifier and had hoped to keep the peace by leaving Yasmin alone behind her bedroom door but, as a child, Yasmin had had no way to find her way back out by herself; she had needed someone bigger and wiser to come in and get her. She had needed to know that her big feelings weren't dangerous and that she didn't need to be left alone until she had calmed down. What she'd needed was a hug from her mum and the reassurance that it's OK, you can't destroy me, your feelings are normal and I can handle them. What she'd needed was some boundaries to help her feel contained in something safe. Instead her mum had backed off and looked the other way.

Care enough to say no

If you please your children as a Pacifier, or as any of the other pleasing profiles, you can give them the wrong impression. You can make them think you don't care enough to put an appropriate boundary in place or say no, or engage in conflict bravely and whole-heartedly. Yasmin's mother had tried to please her by ignoring her challenging behaviour, by doing as she asked and accepting what she said, but in this she had failed her.

I remember working with a teenager who told me that she'd come home after school one day and, after a heated exchange with her parents about her behaviour, they'd confiscated her phone for the week. She'd screamed that she hated them at the time but later came to realise what an unexpected relief it was. For a whole week, she could tell her friends that her wicked parents wouldn't let her have her phone and for a whole week, she didn't feel trapped in a toxic spiral of messaging after school with girls that were spiteful and back-biting. She hadn't had to say no because her parents had done it for her; they had known better than her. I remember when I was growing up, whatever conflict had arisen at school ended at half past three. Locked behind the school gates until the following day, it had room to breathe and could look quite different in the morning after an evening away and a dose of perspective. Nowadays, smartphones in every child's pocket have removed this natural interruption to the drama of puberty and it continues, escalates even, overnight. A child might need their parents to help them to switch off from the turmoil of adolescent relationships from time to time, even if they don't thank them for it. This particular teenager had needed her parents to risk her disliking them temporarily; they'd even let her paint them as the villains in the story to save face at school. Their willingness to be disliked allowed her to regulate herself in the safe space their boundary created for her.

Remember that your kids will have lots of friends, but only one set of parents. Be parents. That means holding boundaries, not where they were for you, or where society would tell you they should be necessarily, but where (often through negotiation) you find a position you can both hold comfortably.

Parenting in the present

How do you feel when you say no to your children?

Maybe you don't like the feeling when you say no, so you do something else instead, you say yes to everything or you fob them off with a 'maybe later'. Maybe you'd feel bad if you said no, or you worry they wouldn't like you, or maybe you want to give them the things that you never got.

It's our job to clean up our boundaries so that we can parent in the present, not in the past and not in an imagined future. We need to say yes when it's appropriate and mean no when it's not.

If we feel guilty or anxious as a result, it's our task to be responsible for resolving those feelings and meeting the need they communicate. We can't meet old needs of our own through giving mixed-up messages to our kids today.

Think back to what it was like for you growing up.

What were you allowed to do? What was off limits or not available? Perhaps there was something that you needed, that you missed out on or you didn't get. Maybe you wish your parents had given you more freedom, or maybe you wish they'd put in more protection. Instead of acting out your unmet needs through your children now, by giving them the freedom or the protection you wanted, give it to yourself.

If you grew up in hand-me-downs or were told to make do and mend, maybe you spoil your kids with toys or gadgets to compensate for your own experiences. I had a client who was a great dad, he'd worked really hard to make something of himself and was a self-confessed 'soft touch', always putting his kids before himself and granting their every wish if he could. One Christmas, he did a beautiful piece of self-parenting when he bought himself the ultimate Lego *Millennium Falcon*, in honour of the little boy who, growing up, had always gone without and could only dream of the toys the other kids had. He knew how to say yes to his kids, but he was only just learning how to say yes to himself.

Go back and meet your past needs if you can, so that you can meet your kids' real needs in the present.

What are you afraid of?

If you have a teenager and you recognise that you aren't comfortable with their behaviour, ask yourself if there's something you're afraid of. The example of Yasmin might sound more extreme than most but, for many parents, it's fear of their child ending up like Yasmin that starts the over-adaptation in the first place. Fear that they'll go off the rails, or turn to drugs, or drop out of school, or self-harm. As adults we can't un-know what we know; we understand the pitfalls and the consequences of mistakes we made or saw others make, so it's only natural that we want to steer our vulnerable adolescents away from danger if we can. The reality is that their experience will be different to yours and you could end up adding the fears from your context to their fears from their own. Parenting from a place of fear isn't good for anyone and our role isn't to prevent our children from failing, it's to teach them the value of mistakes and help them to stumble safely.

Remember that your teenager disliking you isn't only normal, to some extent it's necessary. If they didn't feel the friction they wouldn't have the energy for change, to individuate and launch themselves as citizens of their own states. Fundamentally, they are designed to rebel and they may need to dislike you for a time, in order to be able to leave you. Try to listen to the process rather than the content, the meaning behind what they say rather than the words themselves. The content can be hard to hear because it sometimes sounds personal and as if it's about you, but the process is all about them and their changing relationship with themselves. It's easier to look for the meaning and the need behind their words when we're not feeling floored by the missile they were launched in. Let them know you understand and they'll have the greatest gift – the knowledge that they can separate, they can learn from mistakes and they can be accepted for who they are. Therein lies all the self-esteem and assertiveness they'll need to grow up safely outside the trap of the people-pleaser.

Sadness and the people-pleaser

The inability to tolerate sadness is one of the people-pleaser's biggest drivers. They can't bear to feel others' disappointment so they focus their efforts on making them happy and take some comfort from their joy. They can't bear to feel sadness in themselves and discount it if they can: 'Why dwell on the past when it can't be changed? What if I make other people sad and they leave me? What if I start crying and find I can't stop?'

These pleasers might have had a parent who tried to cheer them up when things went wrong, distracted them or made a joke, hushed their tears or launched into solutions mode. These strategies only served to teach us that we wouldn't be OK if we *did* feel sad, that it must be avoided at all costs or that our sadness is not welcome. The people-pleasing parent passes this baton on to their children. We don't want to be that parent to our children but if we don't repair it, we'll repeat it.

Nobody wants to feel sad, and you'd have to be a masochist to enjoy the heartbreak of loss or the disappointment of expectations unmet, but sad is the most inevitable of the feelings. We will lose and we will be let down and there's no rule we can create around the chaos that grief brings. Because nothing lasts forever and whatever we start will end. And when someone we love dies, or something we love ends, we are designed to feel the impact. It's the impact that tells us it mattered. It's the feeling that motivates us to look for new meaning in life and shows us what to seek going forwards.

If you're sad, forcing yourself not to feel it doesn't make it go away. We need to learn that it's OK to be sad and that the feeling will pass if we let it. If we don't, the sadness can't pass and can force us down unhealthy avenues of distraction and deflection, preventing us from acknowledging our other feelings or noticing our needs.

Our children will feel sad and need this permission too. If you meet your child's sadness with a pained or distressed expression of your own, or brush them off, or jolly them along, they'll learn not to show you their pain. Not that they won't feel it, just that they'll have to handle it alone. They'll learn that their sadness is either dangerous because it makes others sad, or it's not justified and should be ignored. They'll get good at controlling your reaction to them by controlling their own

– the birth of a new people-pleaser and another link in the dependency chain.

If we can't bear it when our children feel sad, we may ramp up our people-pleasing strategies to try to keep them happy, saying yes to every demand, refereeing their relationship battles or pushing a message of positivity where one doesn't belong. If their friend leaves them out of a game it's appropriate for them to feel sad. If they cry when their birthday party ends, that makes sense. If they fail an exam, or get dumped, or a beloved pet dies, we need to make space for their tears. Sad is a natural, healing process for coming to terms with the chaos of the world, and the highs and lows of life and loss. People-pleasing parents may want their children to only feel happy but children will grow up happier overall if we teach them they can also survive feeling sad.

I work with teenagers who have self-harmed as a way out of their sadness or starved themselves to control their painful feelings. Sometimes, not always, what they really needed was a parent who could tune in to them and just be a container for those big and scary feelings, someone they could trust to hold their hand and keep them company in it for a while. There will be times when our children do need a lift, or a distraction or a solution, as well as but not in place of the reassurance that sad is OK, sad is normal, sad will pass. Seeing our children sad can be agonising and we'll need to make space for our own tears too because it hurts to watch them struggle. We might need someone else's shoulder to cry on at these times so that we can be there for our children when they need to cry on ours. It's my belief that we need to let our children see us cry too, not because their sadness is hurting us but because feeling sad is a normal part of life.

Recently we took our two to the cinema to watch the new *Lion King* movie. My husband recounts how he sat at one end of the row, listening to my daughter and I bawling as King Mufasa is sent to his death by the evil Scar, and Simba, just a cub, faces life without a father. As we left the cinema, my daughter, holding my hand and now grinning, turned to her brother and said, 'Well, that was pretty emotional, wasn't it?' It was sad, it was OK, it passed and we moved on.

The next time a movie or a song moves you to tears, practise letting your children see. It might feel uncomfortable at first but you can explain to them that sad's OK, it just tells us that we care. Watching you feel sad and survive will give them the template they need to do the same. You might not please them but you will parent them and that's what they need more.

Parenting yourself around loss

Sadness is the natural response to loss, and the way we respond to sadness now tells us something about how we experienced loss in the past. Sometimes I'll ask clients who struggle with sadness to think about their earliest memory of loss and see what they can remember. It gives me a clue as to what our work will be, in terms of gently guiding them to look behind their defences and come to terms with loss in a way that frees them up to live more courageously and authentically in future. 'Dwelling' on loss doesn't help but nor does moving on too fast, before the feeling has been felt, the loss has been accepted and the meaning has been made.

If you think back to your earliest memory of loss, maybe you can still remember how it felt and what you were encouraged to do.

Maybe it was the death of a grandparent or a pet or the break-up of a friendship, maybe you moved house or changed schools, or it could have been the loss of a beloved possession. Maybe you were encouraged to put it behind you quickly and move on. Perhaps it didn't feel acceptable to talk about it or perhaps you saw that talking saddened the people around you.

Now imagine you got a different message, one that said: 'It's OK, this is sad. I'll keep you company in it. You can take your time. This will pass. You'll be OK.' If you missed out on it back then, you can give yourself the permission and safety to grieve now, and it's a gift you can give to your own children.

We don't want our children to feel sad, but that doesn't mean they won't, and it's not for them to cope on their own or manage our reactions for us. Maybe that's what happened to you in the first place, if you had to manage your parents' feelings for them. It might be a reason why you people-please today.

Pleasing on Special Occasions

For people-pleasers, the true meaning of Christmas is often expense, preparation and stress, and we only cry at our wedding because we're so happy that the planning is over. Occasions that we want to make special come laden with expectations and opportunities to disappoint.

Christmas is a season of goodwill, or so we're told. A time for tradition – defined, as I read recently, as peer pressure from dead people. Whatever your family traditions, you're bound to have felt the pressure that goes with it, the raised expectations and the heightened emotions. Sentimental adverts for department stores begin the conspiracy weeks before, selling a tender vision of homecoming and harmony. Some people-pleasers love Christmas, or at least the idea of it. It presents the perfect opportunity to please but it often falls short in reality. Instagrammed feeds of hand-crafted gifts that cost a fortune to recreate and don't turn out as you hoped. A vision of matching pyjamas on the perfect Christmas morning that can never quite live up to the fantasy. Or the meticulously planned New Year's Eve party that translates into added stress and anti-climax.

Christmas provides a time for reflection, for holding life under a microscope and measuring it against tinselled Facebook feeds. A time to notice more keenly than ever the holes in our happiness or the people missing from our world. It shows us with inescapable accuracy that time is passing and, when we start to count in Christmases, we can't help but understand that life is short, especially if those remaining with our children at home or our parents still alive could be into single figures. Couple this with the notion that it's also meant to be the most wonderful time of the year and there's the rub. Christmas must be magical and so we're left with the mountainous task of being all things to all people, in multiple places at once, with limitless budgets and bottomless cheer. For people-pleasers, Christmas is one big set-up.

If you recognise the disappointment of the Christmas period, it might not be Christmas that's the problem, it might be the expectations you have of yourself that get in the way of you enjoying it for what it really is: another imperfect day on which to please yourself.

Denise

The first therapy session after the holidays is always an interesting one. Clients who left for the break with high hopes of this Christmas being different, come back to tell the tale of its reality. Denise was one of those clients.

When she arrived, she looked dreadful and told me that she'd been in bed since Boxing Day. December hadn't exactly gone to plan and her good intentions for a peaceful Christmas had been drowned out by the noise of her family's expectations. As usual, she had run herself ragged in the weeks before, buying and wrapping the perfect presents, staying up all night rewriting to-do lists and batch-cooking her signature sausage rolls. When Christmas came, she had played the part of the perfect hostess and slaved over not one but two elaborate

Christmas dinners, on consecutive days, with everyone's favourites catered for and a beautifully decorated table that was fit for the cover of a magazine.

After the last guests had left she took to her bed. Completely exhausted, she stayed there for days and as she convalesced, she reflected on what had just happened, how she had done it to herself again. It wasn't about creating the perfect Christmas, she realised, as much as she told herself she did it to make everyone feel special. It was the Pacifier in her that couldn't bear to see the cracks in her family exposed, at a time that was sold to her as a celebration of love and togetherness. In reality, the cracks were always there. Denise's parents had divorced when she was a little girl and she'd dutifully traipsed between two houses on Christmas Day for most of her childhood. She was the glue that held her family together on special occasions and she tried to make them perfect, no matter what the cost.

After she'd finished telling me what had happened, she took a deep breath and smiled. 'Still,' she said, 'at least that's that done for another year.'

I had bad news for Denise. Rather than put it behind her, now was the time to unpick her pleasing patterns and use the rawness of the recent past to guide her towards something better for the future.

Don't miss the meaning

When something goes wrong, or right, we can learn from it if we allow ourselves to reflect. Denise was so relieved that Christmas was over for now that she was about to miss the meaning in her ordeal and leave herself wide open for a repeat performance the following year. The reality is that, for the people-pleaser, Christmas starts at the end of the summer when the first whisperings are made about people's plans and expectations, and it only properly ends sometime in late January once we've recovered from the demands to be festive, and packed away our disappointment with the decorations. That's a big enough proportion of the year to warrant some of your attention in advance. When it comes to special occasions, it's our underlying pleasing patterns that set us up to fail. Understand those ahead of the game and you'll have the means to please yourself and get a result that feels better. Don't be tempted, like Denise, to ignore the issue until the tinsel is back in the shops and the adverts hit your TV screens again.

Christmas by design

Think about last Christmas, or a traditional holiday for you. See if you can remember what it was like, what worked for you and what didn't.

Maybe you found it stressful or exhausting, like Denise, and you can relate to some of the pressures that come with creating the 'perfect' occasion.

If you can recognise that there are parts of Christmas that don't work for you, ask yourself, why do you do them? What are the rules around Christmas in your code? Perhaps your family still expects everyone to be together on Christmas Day, even when the original family unit doesn't exist any more, or perhaps there's pressure to host in the way it's always been done, even when time is short or it feels like a chore. Perhaps you're expected to sprinkle all disagreements with glitter and leave your authenticity at the door, or sacrifice your needs to meet those of everyone else.

Now let's think about how you would like to feel instead.

If you could wave a magic wand, what would your ideal Christmas be like?

Maybe instead of big get-togethers, you crave time off with your immediate family or your close friends. Instead of the traditional Christmas turkey with all the trimmings, you'd love to eat something else. You're tired of swapping presents that nobody wants. Or maybe you'd like to escape the rain and just be on a beach somewhere hot. It doesn't have to be imaginary – you have the power to design a Christmas that works for you. It might not be perfect, but there will be plenty of ways within it to better please yourself.

You might notice that your magic-wand thinking has thrown up an alternative that's perfectly possible with a little renegotiation. Or, you might be aware that your wish list would prove unpopular – maybe it would cause a problem for someone else or provoke a reaction that would feel negative. When we start to please ourselves, we threaten to expose the Christmas conspiracy.

The Christmas conspiracy

Even for families who get along perfectly well long-distance for the rest of the year, Christmas can suddenly throw up a misguided belief that everyone must come together all at once, even when the numbers don't add up. It's unrealistic to have a family of grown-up children, with their own partners, children and in-laws, and still expect to recreate your original unit on Christmas Day. Estranged families, step-families, extended families, families-in-law, all with their own different and subjective traditions, on top of your own ideas and beliefs, can create a heady cocktail of expectations at this particular time of year that is unlike any other. Waiting in the wings is a whole retail sector intent on persuading you that Christmas is meaningful and significant and worth spending all your time and hard-earned money on. Feel-good movies about perfect holiday seasons have a lot to answer for and we are left believing that we have failed if everyone doesn't go to bed on Christmas Day feeling blissful and #blessed. We're told that whatever friction we have felt throughout the year must be ignored because you can't fight at Christmas, and relatives with nothing in common must give up their precious time off work for the sake of a former family ritual. Christmas parties are compulsory, workplace Secret Santas require enthusiastic participation and mince pies must be eaten by the lorryload, whether they give you pleasure or not. These are the socially accepted rules of Christmas and they must be obeyed.

Resistors get through with a 'bah humbug' to tradition but they might miss out on some of the more positive experiences to achieve this blanket opt-out. Pacifiers try to keep everyone happy or avoid tension without a thought for their own needs, whilst Shadows get their pleasure from gift-giving and might struggle to receive. Classics can run themselves into the ground by accepting an invitation to every party and cooking Brussels sprouts in a dozen different ways.

All the profiles have one thing in common: they all try to avoid disappointment. Even the Resistor wants to avoid this painful feeling, so they give up on Christmas before it can let them down. The other profiles might say yes to everything and everyone, for fear of disappointing others. Pleasing yourself means making room for disappointment, en route to something better. Change can be difficult and it can create conflict but it can also herald the start of something great. If nobody likes turkey, it could be time to try something new. If you dread staying in your childhood box room, book a hotel. If you hate high-stakes, enforced-fun parties on New Year's Eve, let yourself mark the new beginning in a way that's right for you – write in a journal or spend time in nature if that's what fills you up. We are supposed to evolve and grow, and tradition shouldn't shackle us to the past, it should be a living story that updates with us. Launch your new traditions for who you are today and let them mould to you, rather than trying to mould yourself to them.

Guilt and the people-pleaser

Sometimes, pleasing yourself means making a choice that upsets someone else. For a people-pleaser, this can trigger overwhelming feelings of guilt.

Guilt is a natural feeling, designed to alert us when we've done something wrong. If we have, then it's pretty simple; the action we need to take is to make a repair, to say sorry or put it right. But what if our action isn't actually wrong, and who gets to decide if it is or not anyway? Maybe we're just guilty of the crime of being ourselves, of having a different opinion or a competing need of our own. Upsetting someone intentionally or carelessly is wrong, but upsetting someone by wanting something different to them is not. In that case, repair or apology won't be the right recourse and no amount of people-pleasing will make us feel relief.

We can reinterpret misplaced guilt as anger turned in on ourselves. If someone dials up their disappointment when we say no to them, it doesn't make us guilty of a misdeed but it may well be grounds for anger at their unreasonable reaction. If we haven't been allowed to feel angry as a child, or to stand up for ourselves, we might not recognise this feeling now. Instead we'll turn it inwards and feel bad for saying no.

The crucial question when we're feeling guilty is: 'Have I done something wrong?' Not according to *their* belief system but according to your own. It is notably not the same as 'Have I had an impact on someone?' or 'Is someone displeased as a result of a choice I have made?' If you notice that you feel guilty around special occasions, ask yourself these questions to work out whether the feeling you have is genuine guilt for doing something wrong, or unfelt anger at an unreasonable reaction that you've turned in on yourself, or sadness at the realisation that you weren't important enough to someone to warrant their respect and understanding. Muddling these reactions can lead to a lifetime of pseudo-guilt that doesn't belong to you. You feel bad for *any* choice you make that has an impact on someone else. You try to avoid it by only living out their choices and never accounting for your own. You can't bear feeling guilty so you have to fall into line.

Pack your bags, you're going on a guilt trip

If someone else uses guilt to control your choices, that's better understood as emotional blackmail or coercion. You have nothing to apologise for but they certainly do. We can't hold ourselves to everyone else's standards, we can only hold ourselves to our own. We can't eliminate our impact on people and nor should we. Impacting on, and being impacted by other people is the basis of human relationships. When we haven't done anything wrong, but someone else is inconvenienced by or disappointed with our choice, the responsibility for resolving that feeling lies with them. People-pleasers are a narcissist's dream and if they prefer to push their needs onto us, it's more appropriate to feel angry than guilty. This is someone treading on your psychological toes, after all; someone claiming that their subjective need is greater, their way is better and their tradition wins. Anger is the healthy feeling we need to restate our boundary and return the responsibility for the need to the person to whom it belongs.

Guilt is a paralysing feeling when it isn't founded in a guilty act, one that our own internal moral compass deems unacceptable. It's a feelings misfire and we can't do anything with it. It's important that we maintain our moral compass and keep ourselves appropriately accountable. We *should* make repair when we find ourselves at the root of a rupture but we can't make amends for a rupture we didn't create. I often hear people-pleasers trying to defend or justify their behaviour, to escape feelings of guilt by converting the other person to their point of view or getting sign-off on their choices. One client told me that his wife was upset when he arranged to see some friends over the holidays: 'She said that I'd decided for both of us that we weren't seeing her family that day then, that I'd imposed my decision on her, but I told her, that's not true! You can still do whatever you want!' I pointed out that, technically, she was right – he *had* made a decision that had an impact on her. But the difference was, he was allowed to. He didn't have to feel guilty, not because she agreed with him but because his behaviour was reasonable. We can acknowledge that our choice is disappointing to someone else but it's not up to us what they do with that disappointment.

The happiest day of your life

Christmas is not the only difficult occasion for people-pleasers. From the most wonderful time of the year, to the happiest day of your life. For a people-pleaser, weddings also offer an endless series of opportunities to disappoint people and feel disappointed yourself, as Amy discovered when it came to planning her big day.

Amy

When Amy got engaged, she was so excited. She bought glossy bridal magazines and read them on her train journey home from work, folding down the corners on pages of beautiful gowns and elegant up-dos. She'd been a bridesmaid before and accompanied friends on their wedding dress shopping trips, drinking prosecco and making encouraging noises as their dreams came true in satin and lace. Now it was her turn, and she eagerly unwrapped her new Bride-to-Be notebook from its cellophane. But she quickly discovered that wedding planning is not much fun for a people-pleaser, and she encountered unsolicited opinions at every turn. Whether it was about the cake, the flowers, the band or the speeches, everyone seemed to have a point of view and an agenda to push.

In her job as a PA she had a reputation for being an excellent event organiser. As a Classic people-pleaser she'd go above and beyond to make things perfect for everyone and could keep even the toughest of crowds happy. This time things were different and she couldn't seem to please anyone. It was as though each of her guests was expecting a personalised party. Eventually, she came to the conclusion that, whilst a cake in itself might be nice, ordering an overpriced, multi-tiered, crowd-pleasing wedding version certainly was not. It was a series of tasks and emails and invoices and, even then, she'd have to listen to how someone else had done it better, in cheese or macarons.

Amy had always known she wanted a small wedding. She didn't want the big affair that her sister had had the year before. She wanted something low-key, something intimate, something where she could feel comfortable and be herself. They found the perfect venue in a cosy converted barn that could take a maximum of forty guests. When her future in-laws emailed with a long list of distant relatives, Amy was horrified. Her fiancé tried to reason with them, pointing out that he wouldn't recognise half of these people in the street, but still they insisted. His parents had been to their children's weddings and they would expect an invitation in return – weren't weddings about family, after all? In the end Amy conceded and booked a hotel conference room that could accommodate the second cousins and the great aunts, but she already felt like she had lost her wedding and was executing someone else's big day.

She busied herself with the invitations. She researched the local hotels and guesthouses, printed maps and directions, and conscientiously tried to cater for every taste and every budget. The replies she received made her feel more like a secretary than the guest of honour. Could she arrange a taxi from the train station? What was parking like at the venue? Did she know if the hotel room had a bath or just a shower? The invitation said it was a child-free event but would it be OK if they just brought the twins?

'If I'm such a people-pleaser,' she said, at her wits' end, 'then where are all the pleased people?'

Her guests felt more like customers, entitled to push their preferences or assert their opinions, far from gracious recipients of her generous invitation.

The guest of honour

People-pleasing hosts need to be aware of the guest paradox they face. The one in which, when you are the guest, your social code dictates that you should show appreciation and accept things as they're offered to you. But when you are then in the position of host, your code also requires you to extend a warm, hospitable welcome, to ask your guests what they would like and adjust your norms accordingly. It's easy for people-pleasers to fall into the trap of deferring to the wishes of others in every situation they come across, never calling bullshit on the contradictions in the code.

When the day came, Amy didn't feel like a bride, she felt more like a party planner. She fixed a smile for the photos but what began as a little girl's dream of a perfect day had become an exercise in stakeholder management. She was well versed in the customs of her own family, but in planning a wedding she'd had a brand-new family to please, one who saw things differently and held different priorities. Then there had been the friends who were more focused on the social event than on the happy couple. She had fallen into the trap of trying to create a day for everyone else and lost the day for herself. When the photobook that she'd ordered finally arrived, she felt sad looking at the bride in the pictures. She'd worked so hard to make everyone else happy that she'd forgotten to please herself.

When two codes collide

Bridal stress, although temporary, is a symptom of deeper issues and emotional baggage. Major life events and significant occasions can expose cracks in existing relationships, triggered by the smallest of practical issues but deep-rooted in complicated family dynamics. It's also a time when different codes collide for the first time as families-in-law bring together their own ideas of tradition and occasion.

Weddings and marriage shouldn't be about making other people happy; in fact they symbolise the ending of a past family and the beginning of a new one, with its own budding codes and customs. Amy gave up her own needs trying to appease people who were all too good at looking out for themselves. Wedding guests aren't stakeholders with a say in the choices you make, but they can't respect your boundaries when you don't set any. If you're planning a special occasion, rather than make reactive decisions under pressure or risk skidding down the path of least resistance, get clear on what matters to you and find your 'no' from the start. If we give up and give in to old, easy pleasing habits, we may feel temporary relief but we deny ourselves the experience we truly seek, to be accepted as we are and connect with others as ourselves.

Perhaps those who don't appreciate the authentic version of you are the ones to let go because there will be plenty who welcome the renegotiation and the opportunity to evolve the relationship. There will also be a precious few who we come to realise already knew the real us and loved us unconditionally.

After her honeymoon, Amy came to realise how people-pleasing had wrecked her wedding and she started to put boundaries in place to take some time for herself. She told me that her best friend had turned up at her flat after several days of unanswered phone calls:

'When I opened the door she started by saying, "Don't worry, I know you want to take time out and I respect that but I just came to give you this." She wrapped her arms around me and gave me a huge hug. With that, she turned around and headed back down the corridor, saying, "Call you tomorrow! And you don't have to answer!" Which she did. And I didn't. I didn't have to please her and it felt bloody brilliant.'

We have to debunk the myth that special occasions are anything more than another opportunity to love and be loved, just as you are. If others tell you that it's a day that matters more than any other, or must incur great expense or be done on their terms, it's simply not true. But it might suit them to have you think so.

The problem with special occasions and their synthetic significance is that they provide a soapbox for others to stand on, fully loaded with hyperbole about the importance of whatever agenda they currently care about. Parties, presents, family time, Christmas cards and credit cards. What matters most is *your* agenda. Not to the exclusion of all others but right at the top of the list. Families can't be held together by a perfect Christmas Day any more than a marriage can be built on Valentine's cards. To demand that you spend time with someone in the way they deem right for *their* reasons, or according to *their* traditions, isn't love and it's not deserving of your energy.

Make active choices

What if we don't want to rupture relationships, or cause conflict on special occasions, even when we can see that the demands they place on us aren't healthy or appropriate? Clients sometimes panic that the only please-yourself alternative is to cancel Christmas altogether or elope to Gretna Green.

Pleasing yourself is really about making active choices that are appropriate, even if those choices aren't necessarily ideal. If, on balance, and accounting for your alternatives, you choose not to rattle the cage at times of artificially heightened emotion or social significance, that's OK and it's not the same as people-pleasing.

We can probably cope with a short, sharp bout of wonky behaviour from others, so long as we can see it for what it is. When you know that it's *their* stuff and it comes from a defensive place of ignorance or insecurity, you can choose to be tolerant if you wish, from an adult place of generosity and empowerment. You may need to limit your exposure by putting boundaries around the total time you spend in these situations and ditching any residual pressures to people-please by reprioritising your own needs when you leave. Acknowledge the post-traumatic fatigue of being around people who don't accept you unconditionally and treat it with a healthy dose of self-pleasing in the days that follow.

If you choose, on balance, to make a time-bound sacrifice for a special occasion, make sure you go into it with fully stocked please-yourself reserves and top up your tank again as soon as possible. No more drawn-out months of politics and people-pleasing in the run-up, no more weeks spent recovering from the fallout and disappointment after the event. If it is to be done, let it be a temporary detour that can be course-corrected quickly with as much, if not more, of the investment and attention that you put into the detour itself.

Prior preparation prevents people-pleasing

If you have a special occasion coming up that feels loaded with pressures to please, how might you manage your boundaries?

Think about what you're willing to offer and give this freely rather than have it demanded from you. Be clear about what you're not willing to do and stick to your guns – it shouldn't come down to a choice between you or them, but if it does, let it be you.

Think about how you will signal to yourself, in the days that follow, that normal please-yourself service has resumed.

Remember, you don't have to take all of you on the day. Think of yourself in parts – there's a grown-up part of you who runs the show day-to-day and a kid part of you who lets you know how you feel. You can leave your 'kid' out of special occasions if it's not safe for them to be there, in other words, if it's not safe for you to be vulnerable.

Denise had a complicated relationship with her step-mother, who was on her own now. She didn't want to cancel their Christmas visit entirely, she just wished she could come away less flattened by the whole experience. We imagined what it would be like to leave her 'kid' outside while her 'grown-up' went in, to exchange some presents and season's greetings.

Metaphorically, she could leave her feelings and her vulnerability out of harm's way and keep them safe on a day when they could be easily hurt by the insensitivity of people she had always tried to please. She just had to remember to pick them up again on her way out and get back to pleasing herself.

Pleasing yourself means treating yourself at least as well as you treat everyone else. Goodwill to all, and that includes you. If people insist you put their needs first, that's not really very festive, is it, and you might be wise to put some boundaries in place to protect yourself when you come face to face on these high-stakes occasions. Even if we're not seeing people in person, we still need boundaries, and perhaps nowhere more so than in the virtual relationships we have online, as we'll see in the next chapter.

Pleasing Online

Instagram, Facebook, Twitter and other social networks offer a hive of potential connections where we can find virtual tribes and be seen and heard in numbers we could never achieve in reality.

There is anonymity and distance online too, and we can take advantage of these to have an authentic voice where we might otherwise feel too self-conscious – a people-pleaser can experience showing up as themselves and feel their view supported for a change. Their opinion, echoed by others, can reinforce their sense of self and validate their beliefs. As a test bed for acceptability, they can garner this confidence to come forward more authentically in real life too. Social platforms can perform a great service for these people-pleasers as well as for the audiences who get the rare privilege of hearing from them. For people-pleasers, to whom acceptability feels important, having a safe space to discover that you already *are* acceptable, without censorship or silence, can be truly liberating. If we broadcast an opinion that secures our standing within our social group, we typically feel more accepted. If we feel accepted, we can feel confident to participate more often, and that is of benefit to ourselves, our key relationships and our wider societies. We can engage confidently in society and be part of something important, purposeful and benevolent.

The problems for people-pleasers online

Online platforms aren't always a force for good, however, and some of the moral outrage expressed online is misplaced and destructive. Social networks combine their relative anonymity with a low risk of repercussion and, under the cloak of invisibility this affords, online users can behave badly and say things they would never say in person. Rather than fulfilling their potential of cooperation and communication across humanity, social platforms can create an environment of pot-stirrers and bullies, one that a people-pleaser reliant on positive affirmation may find too challenging to occupy. Their customary politeness and consideration is not conduct that they can rely on to earn approval online. Their radar, which scans for the responses of their audience, is rendered useless in a disembodied world where nuances of body language, facial expression and vocal intonation are invisible. Online, the people-pleaser is disabled. They can't intuit what's required of them so they can't control the reactions of other people as well as they might in person. Unanswered double blue ticks on WhatsApp leave us bereft, and group chats hold us hostage to the uncensored ramblings of zealous admins and would-be broadcasters, impossible to escape without causing offence should you dare to 'leave the group'.

If the Pacifier pleaser is to foray into this uncharted territory, without their usual antennae to help them manage people's reactions, they'll be forced to show up only as a bland and benign version of themselves, cautiously toeing the party line.

The Classic pleaser must arm themselves with filters and edits, to transform their pictures and posts into something worthy of universal affirmation. They must flood their feeds with inspiring content that their public will applaud, and keep up a supply of positive vibes only. The Shadow pleaser might not be a prolific poster but they will follow and like the posts of influencers they admire, and bombard their DMs with fan-girl adoration. They'll defend their idols against trolls and tag them in their stories, to help them grow their exposure or further their aims. Unable to live and let live online, the Resistor may take themselves off the platforms altogether. They may criticise the posts of others, or dismiss the value of social media in its entirety.

Social media is not inherently positive or negative for people-pleasers; as always, it comes down to our motivations and the way we engage. To please ourselves online, we need to understand why we engage in the way we do.

Anita

Anita was on social networks for all the wrong reasons.

She was twenty-six when she came to see me. She was anxious and wanted to work on her low self-esteem. She told me about her obsession with Instagram, how she would spend hours scrolling through feeds of perfect people eating perfect breakfasts, celebrities with post-workout glows, or her ex-boyfriend on exotic holidays with his suntanned arms wrapped around beautiful girls in bikinis.

Her own uploads were meticulously filtered as she tried to present to the world her most pleasing persona. 'Sometimes,' she told me, 'I'll get myself ready to go out and take literally hundreds of pictures. I'll try out every angle and filter and I feel like the more I take, the worse I feel. Then I'll post one with some message that has to be exactly the right mix of confident and self-deprecating with every hashtag under the sun, #outout, #lovemygirls, #sorrynotsorry ... #me, #happy, #bodyposi-tive, and after all that I might not even go out. I'll just take my makeup off and put my PJs on and watch TV. It's all a lie. Or, if I do go out, I'll spend the whole evening on my phone checking for likes. If it doesn't get enough likes I'll take it down. I hate it. I hate *myself* for doing it.'

Anita hid her face in her hands. She felt embarrassed at her irrational behaviour but she couldn't break the habit of people-pleasing on social platforms. She would google which hashtags would get her more likes or more followers. She would accept unquestioningly the distorted view of other people's lives and feel like a failure next to their perfection. Before she'd even posted her selfie for universal judgment she'd have pre-judged herself unworthy and self-fulfilled the prophecy.

She had used dating apps to look for love and told me about one site that didn't offer you the option to just say 'thanks but no thanks' to someone you'd chatted with online. You had to actively 'blacklist' them. She had been blacklisted by guys she'd messaged, and described how utterly worthless it made her feel. Even when she thought she'd made a connection, a guy could just vanish into thin air after weeks of non-stop messag-ing. This process of 'ghosting' left Anita not knowing what had gone wrong and, typical of the people-pleaser, in the absence of known alternatives she blamed herself. She would imagine the worst about herself and try even harder to please the next person.

Some people, like Anita, find their way onto social networks for the wrong reasons. Their unmet needs in real life lead them to seek a feeling of belonging online and they use their people-pleasing know-how to offer up a polished imposter, rendering any resulting acceptance null and void. Anita used Classic pleasing patterns to seek connection, but you can't get close to a faceless follower. She wanted to feel understood, but you can't be seen if you never show yourself.

Social media motivations

Think about your motivations for engaging online.

Why do you use social media?

Think about what you get out of it. There are likely to be positives and negatives, or wanted and unwanted effects – see if you can account for both.

Maybe social networks give you a way to show up as yourself and gather the evidence that you are good enough, to take with you into your life offline.

Or perhaps you engage online to please other people, and you measure your acceptability by likes, retweets and upvotes.

If that sounds like you, ask yourself how you present yourself.

How do you think the online world sees you and how true to life is the picture you present?

Selfies and posts can be edited and filtered, put out for public polling, removed or upvoted. You can edit yourself and filter yourself, and in the process you can also lose yourself in the dangerous pursuit of 'likes'. You can share memes about feelings without ever expressing how you feel. We can't feel understood if we aren't being true to ourselves, and we can't feel seen if the people seeing us are just pretending too. That's just one imposter 'liking' another imposter. For a people-pleaser, the number of likes, or followers, or comments we receive for our posts has become a dangerous and arbitrary measurement of our likeability and our success, and it could be damaging our mental health.

Fantasy versus reality

Don't make the mistake of comparing your inside to everybody else's outside. It's important to remember that the best life they are living on Instagram is likely not the true picture, or at least not the full picture.

If you look back through your own online profile, the 'outside' you that you have shared with other people, you might notice that it looks like the kind of profile that you could feel intimidated by, were it posted by someone else. You might have commented on something you felt you should, or retweeted something that you'd like to believe but don't entirely. Your outside might sometimes be the social media life that someone else's inside feels inferior to. You might notice that your timeline hides your full truth – perhaps the last story you shared held its usual mixed bag of emotions but the soft-focus photograph you posted was picture-postcard nostalgia and its accompanying message was one solely of positivity and joy. It only tells one side of the story and it's important for everyone, especially people-pleasers, to remind themselves of that. If you can fake it, so can everyone else.

Before you unfollow

If you're someone who takes pleasure from scrolling through beautifully curated feeds, that's great, there's lots of good stuff on social media and much of it can be experienced as positive, uplifting and entertaining. Plus if someone's posts bother you, at least you can block them or unfollow them, right? That's what we're told to do anyway – curate our feed and only follow what makes us feel good.

When I work with clients who are upset by interactions online, I find it more helpful to lean into what bothers them first and listen for what's going on at a deeper level. If we skip this stage and go straight for social media cold turkey, we might calm the symptoms of an underlying issue that only flares up when we view a particular type of post. If we just tailor the content we see in order to remove the triggers, we might bring ourselves temporary relief from the uncomfortable feelings, but we'd be treating the symptoms not the cause. Whereas, if we can understand the feelings, we won't need to dodge them in the future. We might even find that the understanding helps us to get closer to learning how to please ourselves. That's not to say we won't also make changes to the content we expose ourselves to, just that first we need to be clear on our motivation for doing so. We want to feel resilient online, not just soothed in the moment on its ever-shifting sands.

If you don't engage online, take a moment to think about how you might feel if you did. If you avoid social media because you know that spending more time on networks would likely trigger feelings of irritation, or inadequacy, or anxiety, get curious about why that might be and what other action you could take so that you can show up online if you choose to, able to please yourself.

Malik

Malik thought that social media was the problem but it turned out it was the restrictions he placed on himself that were frustrating him.

Malik would talk about how pathetic it was when people posted their hazy still-life shots of coffee cups positioned next to effortfully stacked literary zeitgeists, lit, filtered and broadcast into his feed with an air of self-satisfied entitlement. He'd laugh as he described them but it was clear he felt agitated by the arrogance and vanity they represented.

We didn't have to dig too much deeper to understand that the main perpetrator was a man Malik knew from university who, he believed, carried a misplaced sense of confidence in everything he did. He was in a similar line of work to Malik now and whilst Malik would meticulously research developments at the cutting edge of his field in social science, this guy would publish noisy tweets with half-cocked opinions. Worse than that, he would gain popularity from it, amassing vast numbers of followers wanting to hear more from his virtual soapbox. Malik was tentative and conscientious in his work and had the modest salary to match, whilst this colleague would be booked for lucrative after-dinner speeches and cushy gigs at corporate away-days.

Social media networks had given his colleague a platform from which to wax lyrical about himself and elevate his ego and Malik couldn't bear it. He saw it elsewhere, too; friends boasting about their perfect holidays on Facebook and colleagues posting bragging updates on LinkedIn about their promotions. He would pour scorn on the 'likers' and the 'followers' too, for failing to see through the hot air that was being blown around them.

When Malik described with contempt the latest Instagram post from this colleague, a regurgitated Zen proverb with a dozen blanket hashtags about peace and positivity, we took the opportunity to pause and reflect. Malik had unfollowed him to get away from the feelings, but the friction he felt told us this person represented something significant to Malik, if only we could tune in to what was really going on.

'I guess I'm irritated by him,' he began. 'I mean, what gives him the right to preach this stuff? He thinks he's better than everyone else and that whatever he says is important enough for us all to listen to. And these idiots do listen and they blow smoke up his arse! They feed his ego and he gets all this credit for what? Nothing! That's what I hate about Instagram, it gives megaphones to morons.'

Ideally, Malik wanted his colleague to stop posting so confidently and irreverently but, failing that, he wanted to unfollow him to eliminate his exposure to the posts that annoyed him, or denounce social media altogether. Resistors don't want to care but they do, otherwise Malik wouldn't have been bothered by his colleague's posts and could have scrolled past unaffected. Resistors are just as susceptible to pressures to please but unlike the other pleasers, they don't try to comply with the expectations, they try to deny them or defy them as a means of regaining some control. In all four profiles, there is a lack of agency that means they can't negotiate the way they engage with authority, to self-select only the items of importance. Instead they either opt all-in, like the Classics and the Shadows and the Pacifiers, or they opt all-out like the Resistors. If, as an adult, you still have to defy authority, it might mean you lack your own. This was the real change that Malik needed to make if he was to learn to please himself.

Malik was projecting his own unfinished business onto his colleague. By projection, I mean the process in which we see in someone else something we deny or dislike about ourselves. We are blind to it in ourselves but when it shows up in others we feel aggrieved. The person who sacrifices their own needs in order to perform as a people-pleaser will resent acts of self-interest from others. The person who would never allow themselves to be late will hate tardiness from those around them. The person who wishes they could be less worried about getting it right will struggle with people who seem comfortable to make mistakes.

Malik struggled with a man who acted with authority and conveyed a high sense of self-worth because Malik denied this to himself. Deep down, Malik was angry because he would never dream of imposing his sunrise pictures on the world; he would never believe what he had to say was worth broadcasting to the masses. He had been brought up to have humility and be undemanding of others, and seeing his colleague break these unwritten rules was intolerable. The real change his anger needed to precipitate was not a change in his colleague but a change in himself, from believing he must hide his light under a bushel to allowing himself to shine. Counter-intuitively, Malik needed to take a leaf out of his colleague's book – maybe not the whole volume, but certainly a chapter. He needed to update some of his own childhood rules about being modest and grateful to allow himself to have a voice and set an expectation of others to make room for him.

Feeds of frustration

If you notice that there are feeds that frustrate you, or Facebook friends that trigger an uncomfortable reaction, before you unfollow them, let's first explore what they bring up in you.

What annoys you about the way other people behave on social media?

Perhaps these people give themselves permission to do or be something that you don't allow yourself. Perhaps they assume the value they bring, in a way that you wouldn't feel entitled to. Could this be the change you make instead – to tread more heavily in your own life, with less concern for how you are perceived?

Perhaps their narrative conceals their own insecurities. Maybe you could observe that this is the way they present themselves to the world in *their* bid to organise the reactions they get. Maybe they are actually a closet people-pleaser, following a different code.

If you find yourself feeling frustrated by them, notice that this may not be about you at all. This may be the unwanted reaction they unwittingly provoke in everyone and it's about their relationship with themselves. If this is the case, you might come to a place where you can view their messages with more compassion, or at least not feel so affected by them. You might be able to get out from under that original pressure to defy or comply with the authority they represent and instead understand it as a hangover from their early conditioning, as we saw in the chapter on pleasing your parents. They can go back to

being just a person with their own stuff and their own
blind spots, no greater than or less than you, and you can
go back to getting on with your life, being and doing
whatever's appropriate for you.

Leaning in to the material online that you find difficult might
be more enlightening than simply culling it from your feed, if
you're willing to look beneath your initial reactions and
understand the feelings that it brings up and the rules that it
challenges. Maybe it's time to update your permissions and
give yourself the same freedoms that you see other people give
to themselves, to be seen and to be heard. Pleasing others, or
alternatively removing yourself from pleasing platforms, will
only keep you stuck in the limited permissions you received as
a child.

Cold turkey

We can learn a lot about ourselves and our relationships with
others by observing what bothers us online. We can also learn
from observing what bothers us about *not* being online.

Imagine what it would be like if you uninstalled all your
social media apps or went cold turkey for the day. How might
you feel? Perhaps you'd miss the comments or likes you receive
when you post something popular. Acceptance based on popularity or polish is conditional and, if we are only OK when we
meet a set of conditions, we're not really OK at all. The only
OK-ness worth having is unconditional OK-ness, being loved
and accepted as we are with no strings attached. Sometimes we
have to go through a painful period of giving up our conditional acceptance first, to make way for the unconditional

acceptance that can follow. You might have to stop posting an over-filtered online version of you, and lose the likes that go with it, to find out that you can engage online as the real you and tolerate the liking *and* the disliking this brings. You can cope with both, so neither need drive you.

Perhaps you'd feel bored or cut off without your phone and screen time is a way to fill the gap. People often reach for their phones without stopping to ask themselves why, or what it is they need. Imagine for a moment that boredom is a cover-up feeling, masking some other, more authentic feeling of which you may not have been aware.

Cover-up feelings

Boredom tells us our needs aren't being met somehow. It tells us when we're not satisfied or stimulated but it doesn't provide the useful energy we'd get from anger to make a change, nor does it give us the important reflectivity from sadness to point us towards making more of our real-life connections. It's a cover-up that triggers us to reach for a distraction instead of a resolution, and I often hear it from people-pleasing clients who weren't encouraged to act on their authentic feelings as kids. That kid who was bored at the back of the class wasn't messing about because he was naughty, he was distracting himself because he had a need that wasn't being met, be it for a different way of learning, a break, or some help with regulation. Similarly, when clients tell me they feel tired or flat or numb, I'll ask them, if they weren't feeling that way, how else might they be feeling, what would their real need be? Aside from physical tiredness from increased activity or sleep deprivation, people will often come to notice that fatigue, for example, is more about feeling frustrated, stuck, lonely or sad.

Anxiety is another common cover-up feeling that I see in people-pleasers who come to therapy. It shows up as the difference between expectation and reality, how we want things to be versus how they are. When we aren't able to accept things as they are but we don't believe we can change them, anxiety forms an uncomfortable bridge between the two. All four of the pleasing profiles can suffer from anxiety as they draw on different tactics to make situations tolerable without a sense of genuine agency or control.

I invited Anita to tune in to her feelings of anxiety and ask herself a different question: 'If I wasn't feeling anxious right now, what might I be feeling?' If anxiety didn't always show up as that first-response emergency feeling, what might she feel instead as she looked at the pictures of people living their best lives? For Anita, the anxiety was masking a feeling of deep loneliness. She went online feeling bad and she came off feeling worse. It was the loneliness that required her attention; the anxiety was just there to bring her attention to it.

Anxiety is a particular problem for the people-pleaser and we can easily seek out online affirmations in a bid to feel better, but presenting a fragile online identity to be scored by an audience of ten-second scrollers is likely to make you feel more anxious, not less. Whether people-pleasers feel anxious and so look to social media, or whether people-pleasers look to social media and so feel anxious, the effects appear to be correlational. Looking to social networks can make you feel low and feeling low can make you look to social networks.

What lies beneath?

If you reach for a phone and start to scroll when you feel bored, anxious, or low, see if you can notice what authentic need you might be distracting yourself from.

You may recognise that your online interactions help you avoid some other, more uncomfortable feelings and it may be that you missed out on some of the permissions you needed to please yourself in the beginning. You've got the opportunity now to replace your cover-up feelings with authenticity and resilience. If your options to date have been to freeze or to please, you may not have had permission to lose, or fail, or fall, and get back up again, shame-free and supported. This is a permission you can give yourself now.

If, having explored your motivations for using social media, you recognise yourself as a 'social' online user, by which I mean you're in control of your consumption and you generally enjoy your interactions, that's great, but you might still be wise to take some sensible precautions to protect yourself online. Be selective in who you connect with, limit how much of yourself you put out for public consumption, and take the opportunity to share your real self as a test run for your unconditional acceptability in real life. When you feel pulled to people-please online or pull the plug, step back and observe your triggers, using your authentic feelings to reset your boundaries. This is pleasing yourself online.

If, however, you recognise that you're using social networks and online platforms more compulsively to prop up your fragile self-image, and your inner people-pleaser has an unhealthy relationship with the likes and follows you receive, avoiding triggers of irritation or anxiety won't be sufficient. Before you engage on social media according to the norms of others, check whether these are also your norms. And if you're someone who says 'social networks aren't for me', notice whether you might be missing out on their potential to avoid their rules of engagement.

Let your behaviour online be a reflection of who you are offline and don't fall foul of the pressure to be perfect. When you please yourself on social media, you allow like-minded individuals to meet the real you, #no filter, and build an online community where you can feel welcome, just as you are.

Pleasing as a Woman

I am often asked if people-pleasing is a female affliction. In my experience I would say no, although some of the more stereotypically female traits may lend themselves to some of the more stereotypical pleasing strategies. Remember that, at its core, people-pleasing isn't about being caring, it's about organising the reactions of other people to avoid a feeling you don't want. There's nothing exclusively female about that. The element that could potentially feel more 'female' is the unconscious need to not make a fuss or put anyone out, to seek harmony or support the gains of someone else, even when it comes at great personal cost. People-pleasing isn't gendered in the traditional sense of the word and it affects us all to some extent. You may recognise your people-pleasing patterns within the case studies of the women in this chapter, you may recognise yourself in those of the men in the chapter that follows, or you may recognise yourself in both.

Sugar and spice

It is true that females are conditioned in many cultures to be caregivers, to prioritise others and be helpful. Praised for being sweet and biddable, little girls are often told not to be bossy or to make a fuss. The female brain is typically wired for greater empathy than the male brain and this can be a great strength, enabling women to build strong, pro-social relationships and collaborative communities. It falls down when it lacks the permission to also have boundaries, to feel and express anger, and to treat yourself as well as you treat everyone else. Sometimes I'll ask my female clients, amid a monologue of negative self-talk and sabotage, 'What would you say if someone spoke about your best friend this way?' Often the answer is along the lines of: 'I'd be furious! I'd say, how dare you speak about her like that!' This is the pivot a people-pleaser needs to make, to turn her beam of care and protection back towards herself, to rediscover the feelings of anger that were conditioned out of her (by both men and women) and to use it to tell people when to step off.

The pleasing woman is often stereotyped as the one who spreads herself too thinly, seeking the approval of those around her and never saying no. She is a devoted daughter, a loyal friend, and a dedicated employee. She manages the family calendar and the household duties, buying the birthday presents, restocking the cupboards and scheduling the social activities. She takes responsibility for schools, friends, holidays, pets and in-laws, on top of her own career and obligations. This is the woman who feels like she's failing if one of the myriad plates she spins should smash. The woman who feels like she can't succeed at work unless she's saying yes to her boss. The woman who feels like a nag if she complains about the unfair division of labour at home. The woman who feels like a bad mother if she opts for a shop-bought birthday cake.

You might have been raised to a different pleasing code; perhaps the females in your family were supposed to be strong and dependable, you didn't get the message to be meek, and your own please-yourself journey might be one of reclaiming your vulnerability. Whether you relate more to the women in this chapter, or the men in the next, look for the lessons they learned and see what might be meaningful for you.

The Viking way

My primary female role model was a Viking. In my culture, women weren't fragile or inferior, they were strong and independent. Equal to men, if not ever so slightly more capable and that bit more resilient.

When I look at grainy photographs of my mother, arrived from northern Sweden in the early Seventies, I see long brown braids, red clogs and biceps. When she was heavily pregnant with my brother, my father came home from work to find her hauling a discarded manhole cover up the driveway. 'Could come in useful,' he remembers her saying, barely breaking a sweat.

My clothes were well made and practical, primary-coloured corduroy run up in her sewing room under the eaves. My shoes were sturdy and made for being outdoors in all weather. There were many times that I longed for frilly pink party dresses and patent leather shoes, yet I find myself repeating history with my own daughter now – sending her to school in hard-wearing, waterproof trainers with a good grip, so that she can get on with the games at break and not be slipping around in the shiny Mary Janes I see on the feet of her friends.

It's important to me that she be able to stand on her own two feet (quite literally), but being able to support herself doesn't mean she must support everybody else.

My clients are invariably courageous, capable, emotionally intelligent and resilient women. Some, however, were only taught to use their abilities in service of others, and hold the mistaken belief that it is their duty to share their resources with people who might need them, even when they don't deserve it.

Amber

Amber had been conditioned to be a pleasing female. She had a younger brother who had determined every game they would play as children, allocated her the role of Robin to his Batman and goalkeeper to his penalty practice. When she grew up and made her own friends, she realised that she didn't want to play his games on his terms any more. Her mum would say, 'But you should want to play with your brother – he just wants you to play because he loves you.' She felt like the fly in the family ointment and as though, if those were the conditions of loving relationships, she had to find ways to mould herself into the right shape and receive love in the way it was offered. She'd go back to playing his games, begrudgingly moving around an army of plastic soldiers or sitting in a den of his design. For years she Shadow pleased to facilitate his days in the sun but she felt resentful and developed Resistor patterns to limit the time they spent together.

Decades later, Amber found she still had plenty of conversations like this. Admittedly not about dens any more but still about delivering everyone else's dreams: hen dos, family visits, work socials, school fundraisers, book clubs, birthday parties, weddings or dog walks. So many requests to grant the wishes of other people, and a deep-seated discomfort at the prospect of letting them down, equating this with the belief that she was being cruel or uncaring if she said, 'No thanks' or 'Not for me'. The list felt endless and she came to therapy at the point that she'd finally 'burnt out' and made an appointment with her GP. She'd been surprised when he suggested counselling.

We started by exploring what happened for Amber when a friend or loved one wanted her to do something:

'Every time I get invited to something, it's like I go into a state of turmoil ... I wrestle with myself about whether I *ought* to go, whether I *want* to go, or even whether I *ought to want* to go!' She laughed at the impossibility of her inner taskmaster. 'I think about whether I owe them a yes this time or whether I've got a good enough reason to say no. How I *actually* feel never really comes into it.'

She would haul herself over the coals, asking: 'Why do I never want to do stuff? I like this person, it could be fun and I'll probably enjoy it once I'm there ... what's *wrong* with me, why am I so antisocial?' Always back to the same question. 'What's wrong with me?' Whether she eventually accepted or declined the invitation, she'd feel bad either way.

Making yourself a priority

Amber had been brought up by a mother who modelled to her that being female was about being caring and accommodating, amenable and understanding. In Amber's family, if you were female then you put others first. When it didn't work for Amber to keep blindly pleasing as an adult, she didn't doubt the integrity of the code, instead she doubted herself.

What Amber wanted most was to hear someone say, 'Hey, I'd love to see you, let me know if there's something you'd like to do, and when it would suit you to do it.' That would be the bullseye that said she was finally important enough for someone to have a relationship with on terms that worked for her as well, that took account of her and didn't require her to help someone else deliver their own agenda or avoid their own difficult feelings. That said she wasn't an afterthought, or a prop or a placeholder. Amber found her anger at last – she recognised she was cross with the friends and family who guilt-tripped her into seeing them because *their* lives were unfulfilled; she was fed up with being a means for her managers to trick her into doing extra work with the great 'development opportunities' they'd offer her.

As long as we accept these dysfunctional, conditional relationships, we prevent the ones we really want from ever coming our way. If you take the emotional responsibility for everything, from everyone, this will likely be what you're given. If you seek to solve every problem you're presented with, problems will inevitably land on your lap. If you want a job done, give it to a busy woman, right? If she's busy it's probably because she's already doing everybody else's work for them and so she won't say no to doing yours. That's the value she believes she brings and what people will come to her looking for. She'll do it because she's good at it, or so she's been told, but just because she can do it doesn't mean she should.

Amber's mother had praised her when she took care of her brother and let him have his own way. In therapy she came to understand that it had probably been helpful for her mother to have someone else to share the responsibility with – she too had found it hard to entertain him in the ways that he demanded. In this way, Amber's mother had taught her, albeit unconsciously, how to prioritise the needs of others, particularly males, over her own, according to her own code of female conditioning. She had been hoodwinked by her mother into pleasing her brother and she felt resentful towards them both, for manoeuvring her into positions that suited them. The guilt she felt if she denied them their wish was really anger that she'd turned in on herself.

Maybe, like Amber, you wonder if there's something wrong with you, if you prefer an evening in with the company of Netflix or an early night, instead of drinks after work. Or if you feel lacklustre when you're invited to a party or a weekend away with friends. Or if you feel stressed when your boss offers you an exciting high-profile project to lead. Maybe you too measure yourself against what other people want and discount your own inclinations.

Female conditioning often leads women to believe that their own needs aren't valid, or are a nuisance to others. They act in service of others and forget to act in service of themselves.

Following the female code

Think back to the rules around gender that you experienced when you were growing up.

What did being female mean in your family?

Perhaps little boys and little girls were treated differently, or there were different expectations. Maybe you can remember some of the messages you got, directly and indirectly, from the women who raised you through the roles they performed in the family.

Were there feelings or behaviours that were unacceptable for females when you were growing up? Was it different for the males?

See if you can notice how these rules still play out in your life today.

Feel free to make a fuss

I work with a lot of women who were conditioned with the belief that they shouldn't inconvenience anyone and that to change your mind is somehow giddy or capricious. You must predict ahead of time how you'll feel two weeks on Thursday and RSVP in blood. Sure, there may be some things that can't be so easily undone, maybe tickets have to be bought or babysitters booked. But mostly things can be rearranged, repair can be made, or an apology offered. Give yourself permission to change your mind. It's not 'making a fuss', and you'll be amazed how easy it is and how respectfully people can respond. If you realised how little time people spent thinking about you, you might not worry so much about what they thought.

There is a caveat to this, however. The option to change your mind doesn't mean you can say yes in advance with a sneaking suspicion that you'll bail on the day. That's just the sugary hit of short-term people-pleasing with a bitter aftertaste of disrespect. That's just you prioritising your desire to feel liked *now* over the other person's right to reasonable consideration. If you can't be certain, it's OK to use other words: 'I like the sound of it but I don't know how I'll feel at the end of a busy week at work, so can I let you know nearer the time?' Or 'It sounds lovely but I'm on a budget this month so I won't say yes yet – when do you need an answer?' Equally, if your answer is no, it doesn't have to be delivered brutally: 'It does sound fun but it's not really my thing,' or 'I'd love to see you but I need to hibernate for a bit, I'll message you when I resurface,' or 'I'm saving my money for something else right now.' If the other person cares about you, that will be good enough. If not, maybe they are a bit like Amber's brother, unconsciously more interested in getting their own needs met than being in an equal relationship with you.

Know your own mind

Some women missed out on the permission to be disagreeable or to create friction in early relationships. They have a predisposition to accept things graciously and be grateful for gestures of kindness, whether they want what's offered or not.

Maybe you would like to say yes to an invitation from a friend but you'd prefer a walk and a coffee together, rather than the cocktails they suggest. Maybe you would love to watch a film with them or have a glass of wine together at home. It's OK to have your own idea of fun and for that to be different from what someone else enjoys. It might even be what your friend would prefer too but they are caught up in their own accepted social code of what makes for a 'pleasing' evening.

Maybe the progression you would like at work is not the high-profile, public-speaking opportunity you've been offered but you would like to mentor members of the team or develop the strategy. In our extrovert-biased world, we can find ourselves coerced into people-pleasing on a social scale and we need to be able to make our own contribution, on our own terms.

As always, the other person might say no; that's a possibility a people-pleaser has to face when they start to please themselves, but one that is recovered from more quickly, and with less harmful side effects, if it's tackled in the moment.

Amber was told that it's the thought that counts and that, if someone means well, you're duty bound to accept their relationship. This is a particularly dangerous message for women, raised to believe that 'it's nice to be nice' and that to say no to a friendly offer is unkind, even when it's potentially harmful.

Amber struggled with people-pleasing in a way that is all too common among the women I see. Dilemmas that look like the lighter sides of female people-pleasing are often dismissed with frothy flippancy as the problems of being 'too nice' or needing a bit more 'me time'. Not only does this diminish the damaging impact on the individuals in these situations, it also forms the thin end of a denigrating wedge that masks the most sinister impacts of female people-pleasing, and the way it leaves the door ajar for women to be physically and emotionally abused.

Abusive relationships

There's a spectrum of dysfunctional relationships. At one end, there might be the needy friend who messages you every day. Since this can be draining at times, you take rain checks and find creative ways to help them feel loved from a distance. Their demands can be exhausting but, overall, aren't ill-intentioned. At the other end of the spectrum lies more pathological manipulation, people who coerce other people into behaving in ways that advance their own agendas. This can happen in friendships but I'm thinking particularly of the risk in romantic relationships. Those relationships where they put you through hell and call it love.

In these situations, people-pleasers can feel a duty to receive love in the way it is offered and to sidestep bad behaviour because they've been told 'it's the thought that counts'. It isn't. If someone repeatedly treats you badly, lets you down, or abuses you, the thought categorically does not count and only the actions do. At the extreme end, a stalker could even believe their actions to come from a place of love. A client recently told me she had stayed in a domestic violence situation because 'when he's nice, he's wonderful and he puts me on a pedestal'. A pedestal is not a place you ever want to be. It might sound flattering if you're a people-pleaser seeking validation but it actually means you find yourself restricted to a tiny platform of existence, forced to control your movements and ration your responses, for fear of a painful plummet. Only behaving in a people-pleasing, pedestal-worthy way will keep you at your lofty heights and safely away from the edge.

If you find yourself on a pedestal, bring yourself down to earth quickly by letting the other person hear how you really feel and know that, if they don't want a relationship with you on an equal footing, it was never the right relationship. Delaying that fall from grace by trying to please them will only train them to expect it, making the inevitable landing all the harder when it comes. If you mould yourself into a position of accepting love in whichever way it's offered, you forget the important step of self-selecting which kind of love you want to receive. Refusing 'love' from someone who offers it in a manipulative, ulterior or controlling way is not unkind, it's self-preservation and it's vital for pleasing yourself.

Lena

Lena had always had a tricky relationship with men. From the very beginning she'd felt it was her responsibility to keep them happy. Her father was inconsistent with his affection; sometimes she was in favour and at other times he could be punitive and rejecting, favouring her sister over her.

As she grew up and began dating, she found that she seemed to attract a lot of male attention, especially from men who wanted her to please them. She'd accept their initial offer of a drink but end up dating them for months or even years, feeling guilty for not liking them as much as they seemed to like her. She couldn't keep it up forever and when eventually she called it a day, they'd be mortally offended and accuse her of leading them on.

Eventually she began to avoid men altogether in a bid to dodge the quid pro quo that she'd learned to expect at the end of every conversation. Their initial compliments and chivalry always seemed to create an expectation in her, even an obligation, to return the favour. It got so bad, she told me, that she found herself in a blind panic on the street one day, when her shopping tumbled out of her broken bags and a passing man stopped to help. 'I froze! All I could think was what was he going to expect in return? I'd read all these horror stories online about men offering to carry your bags home and then attacking you so I just left my shopping on the pavement and ran!'

Being by herself felt safe, but she was lonely and her friends were all starting to settle down. In the end, her best friend convinced her to try internet dating but her sense of obligation to keep men happy only became more apparent, and she came to therapy to get to the bottom of it once and for all.

She started by telling me about the most recent guy she'd dated. 'He seemed perfectly polite, buying me drinks and asking me questions, but as the evening went on I just felt more and more uneasy, so I made an excuse and pretended I had a migraine. He was clearly concerned but I said no when he offered to drive me home. I just faked a smile and kissed him on the cheek, said thanks for a great evening and promised we'd rearrange. By that point I just wanted to get out of there.' When I asked her what had made her feel so uncomfortable, she told me she couldn't put her finger on it. As we explored it, she came to realise what her unconscious was wary of: 'I think it was because he seemed so keen and I didn't want to disappoint him. I was scared. When he asked if I wanted to meet again, I said yes, even though I didn't. I just wanted to keep things light and friendly between us so that he'd let me leave and not cause a scene. I thought he'd be angry with me if I told him I wasn't interested.' Unconsciously, Lena held on to the belief that if she displeased any man he would get angry with her, and she had been conditioned to think that it was her responsibility not to provoke them. As a Pacifier, she would turn her fear into people-pleasing and adapt herself to keep them sweet.

Lena never wanted to upset or anger a man because, on some level, she was scared he might attack her. Her father had let her down here, leading her to believe it was up to her to manage him, making it her job to shape herself around his unpredictable moods and elicit a reaction that felt safe. She'd never found fault in him, or any other man – only in herself. She feared provoking their anger, when she should have been feeling her own.

We'd never know for certain whether her instincts were right about the guy on this occasion and she never did rearrange their date, but it's crucial that we allow ourselves to act on our feelings and she did the right thing by leaving a situation that felt unsafe. Unlike the people-pleasers who were trained out of their intuition and so inadvertently put themselves in harm's way, Lena's intuition was running into overdrive and told her to fear relationships with men altogether, pre-judging them all as dangerous and volatile. I certainly didn't want to dull her intuition but I did want to help her to update it, and our work would become about unscrambling some of the old signals she'd received, so that she could feel more present and empowered on dates in the future.

Anger is energy for change

Amber developed Resistor patterns to limit her exposure to the pressures to Shadow please her brother, and Lena would deploy her Pacifier when she felt threatened by men. Limiting their exposure to danger or dysfunction offered a partial solution of sorts, but it relied on finding ways *around* rather than through the problems.

To find a meaningful way *through* conflict we have to channel anger as energy for change, in order to set a boundary and say no to unacceptable behaviour. Female people-pleasers have often been raised without the permission to be angry and have tried to get by on socially acceptable feelings of fear instead. Unable to confidently engage in conflict, like Lena, they must use feelings of fear to help them avoid it. The anger that was deemed dangerous or unacceptable is replaced with benign fear or dismissible anxiety. Little girls who were allowed to be scared of boisterous boys (but not allowed to be angry with them) become women who still feel fearful around dominant males and have lost touch with their original potency and ability to self-preserve. If we can only act on fear, we can only hope to get away from a toxic situation, settle for changing ourselves whilst letting the bad behaviour go unchallenged.

Anger is the transformative energy that will help you stop pleasing other people and start pleasing yourself. So far, we have seen how trapped anger can lead to resentment or guilt and how it is actively discouraged in pockets of society. When I talk about anger, I don't mean the destructive temper or violence that hurts others or damages ourselves. I don't mean the resistance or negativity that we self-perpetuate when we rage against the system or hold on to a grudge. I'm talking about the clean, simple unit of feeling that flickers in us when someone crosses our boundary. I'm talking about the friction we feel when something is not working for us and the crackle that gives us the energy to change it. Anger is only ever supposed to signal change. A baby's first communication is a form of this primal change energy: she cries when she needs her parent to alter her state – a feed, a cuddle, a change of clothes. Make the change, and the crying goes away. In this way, to protest is our first line of self-preservation. Without anger as a signal for change and a means of self-preservation, we are at the mercy of the other person's good behaviour, or their ability to read minds, and that's neither a smart nor a safe place to be. We have to hope that they will do right by us, even when as grown-ups we don't do right by ourselves.

Anger is often presented negatively as something to be 'managed' but that's not the case. Rage is destructive, violence is unacceptable but appropriate anger is good for your health. It's a feeling, not an action. It's a regular part of my job to reset the messaging around anger that pleasing women once received. To reset for the little girl that, far from anger being dangerous or ugly or destructive or pointless, its function is perhaps the most important of all the emotions. It tells us when something needs to change.

Anger is your friend

See if you can remember what role anger played at home when you were little, who expressed anger and who didn't, and what you learned to do with your angry feelings.

What were you taught about anger when you were growing up?

Maybe you remember that there was a different rule for boys and girls, Boys could fight but girls could only cry. Angry girls were 'bossy' while angry boys had 'leadership potential'. Maybe only the grown-ups were allowed to get angry, or maybe anger in your household felt scary. Many female people-pleasers confide in me the lengths they go to in order to shield other people from angry feelings, their own and others'. Anger doesn't feel safe and often these women have felt the impact of angry parents in their own past. Grown up, they persevere in toxic relationships or punishing jobs, pouring oil on troubled waters to maintain an anger-free status quo.

Maybe nobody did anger in your family and everyone buried their frustrations or went floppy in the face of adversity. As an adult, you try to problem-solve every scenario with diplomacy and compassion. You avoid confrontation and abandon your right of reply.

All understandable and well-intended tactics to bring peace, but vastly limited and unrealistic when the laws of the jungle are applied. There's a reason why animals with big teeth don't often have to defend themselves. Let people see that you have teeth and you'll find you won't have to use them. Give yourself permission to *feel* anger, and you won't have to act on it, because your boundaries will be clear and they will command respect.

If you weren't taught that it's OK to feel anger and it's OK to have teeth, give yourself that message now. Don't keep your anger on the bench. Felt cleanly and appropriately, anger deserves to be warmed up and on the pitch. It's your first and best line of self-preservation. In order to please yourself, you need to believe you are worth standing up for. You need to believe you're important enough to have a voice when you have something to say, and to show people your teeth when you need to.

Give yourself the message that you matter, that you deserve to be treated well and that you have options for change if someone treats you badly. Use anger as a feeling that patrols the perimeter of your sense of self and spots when your boundaries are being intruded upon. Let its energy for change serve to reinstate your boundaries and preserve your integrity.

Perhaps someone has intruded recently. Ask yourself what you need to do to reinstate a boundary that feels appropriate, remembering that minds can be changed, decisions can be updated and contracts can be renegotiated. Perhaps you've said yes to something and you wish you'd said no. Circle back and find a way to say no now; it's not making a fuss or being flaky, it's authentic and human: 'I know that I said I would but I've reflected on it since then and I've realised that I should have said no. I didn't want to hurt your feelings at the time and I'm sorry if that's disappointing.' Or perhaps you never set a boundary to begin with and that's the place to start. Healthy anger in action is respectful and assertive energy for change. People-pleasing females who have been conditioned out of feeling anger have been left woefully undefended against abuses of power, reliant instead on pleasing strategies and adaptation to keep themselves safe in a world full of sharp teeth.

The female fallacy

Women who sacrifice their career, their friendships, their freedom and their identity to please other people further the belief that this is what it is to be female – to be self-sacrificing and to live in servitude. Feminist teaching can't paper over the behaviours that we observed from the women who brought us up. Even if we act in opposition to our people-pleasing females, we back ourselves into a Resistor corner, caught in rebellion against women from the past and still not free to please ourselves. Women today must unpick the conflicted messages of the women that went before, the generation of mothers who rallied for future females but went home as the dutiful women they'd been conditioned to be. Their confusing message, to be who they wish they were, is not as liberating as the message to simply be yourself.

Right now, to be pleasing to other women might look like being a good feminist and joining the sisterhood, suffering together under the patriarchy and allying with strangers in distorted straw-man arguments. In the cases of the women I work with, there are often as many instances of bad behaviour from women as there are from men. Women who have trampled other women on their way up the ladder or humiliated them to garner popularity; women who have judged each other's choices as a daughter, a friend, a professional, or a mother. We can't locate the female pull to please solely within misogyny when it was the women who raised her that paved the way, and her fellow females that kept her in line.

If you are a female people-pleaser now, notice the messages and models you are setting for little girls growing up today. I hear many of my female clients talk about the guilt they feel as mothers, for going to work or choosing to have an identity outside of their children. They feel bad that they aren't stay-at-home mums baking flapjacks and ironing school uniforms. They feel bad that they choose to go out with their friends instead of listening to the grunts of their teenagers. They feel bad for being tired and snappy at the end of a long week instead of endlessly patient and attentive to their partner. Of course there's a balance to be struck, but feeling bad for not being a 'perfect' partner or mother sends a message down the line that there even is such a thing – a woman who can have it all and be pleasing to all people, who puts herself at the bottom of the pile and never feels frustrated, whistling a happy tune to herself as she shuts up shop on another fulfilling day of delighting everyone. This is the dangerous lie that leads the next generation to expect the same of themselves, or worse, expect it from the women they go on to have relationships with.

Let children experience a real woman who can please herself as well as care for them and they'll get a please-yourself model by osmosis. Stop feeling bad about not being pleasing enough yourself, and you'll break the chains for them. Similarly, be careful if you burden your daughter with sexist anti-male stereotypes. Giving her the responsibility to wage war against the patriarchy sets her up as a future Resistor, a woman locked into a pattern of defiance that leaves her no more free to authentically please herself today than the people-pleasing females that went before her.

I have a son who is nine and his confusion breaks my heart when he watches *Britain's Got Talent* and asks, 'Why does everyone cheer for girl power? Why not boy power? Or just power?' When he comes home from school and his female classmates have told him his goal doesn't count because he's a boy, or that he can't be angry when they are cruel to him because they are girls and that's not allowed. I wince when 'assertive' mothers buy their little girls T-shirts emblazoned with slogans like 'Girls Run the World' or 'The Future is Female'. We're in danger of launching a generation of little girls tasked with avenging past victims, and little boys stung with the punishment of past crimes. It would be a truly strong female who could step outside of her gendered past and campaign for strong, empowered girls *and* boys.

The impact of patriarchy is felt by women *and* men, men who can't conform to its rigid and outdated rules and who don't meet its withering conditions, who don't have a meaningful membership in either camp and find themselves apologetically retweeting feminist memes and burying their own nuanced experiences. Boys and men have suffered too, under the emotionally restrictive rules of archaic masculinity, and require the same permission to be themselves, as we'll explore in the next chapter.

Pleasing and Masculinity

I see a range of pleasing patterns in the males I work with but they're not always as immediately apparent as the long-suffering, plate-spinning, self-deprecating female stereotypes, although these certainly exist too. Sometimes in order to please his tribe of fellow men, a man will have to actively be *not* nice. He must engage in friendships that are based on banter, piss-taking and competition. At work, he must be ruthless and challenging, without needs or vulnerability. In his family he must protect, provide and problem-solve. Different codes from different masters, but often with one aspect in common: a lack of permission to feel. Instead, he must only think or do his way through life. He must be strong, successful and respected. He must be confident, decisive and direct. In some cases, he must even be disagreeable to earn his stripes. A different spin on pleasing but equally founded on a fear of failure and tribal rejection.

Now he is also told he must 'check his privilege' and make sure he is not inadvertently dominating the females around him. Necessary, yes, but also sad and somewhat reductive, given this privilege is a product of the same patriarchal system that has restricted men emotionally for centuries. Little boys who followed this code and learned to bury their vulnerability can go on to become scarier and more dangerous versions of themselves when they grow up, still only knowing how to get their needs met through coercion and control. Especially when they meet the grown-up little girls who were taught to be fearful of conflict and became women unable to express anger themselves, or deal with its emergence in others.

I see many men who struggle with the desire to please others, often failed in some way by their earliest relationships and lacking the ability to form healthy relationships as adults.

Idris

Idris tried to keep people happy. He wanted to be a good man, to make his family proud and be a success at work. He worked hard and enjoyed his job, played sport at the weekends and socialised with his friends. As is so often the case with the men that I work with, everything was fine until the day it all fell apart. The code that he'd always followed, to hide his feelings and discount his needs, failed him when he hit a crisis in his marriage and had no way of coping. Without the maps he needed to meaningfully navigate emotional distress, he could only distract himself from his pain and plummet down rabbit holes of self-destruction.

He came to therapy because his life had finally unravelled. He'd been caught having an affair and even though his wife wanted to work things out, he felt he couldn't go back. He'd tried for a while to keep both women happy, denying the existence of each to the other, spinning a web of lies that kept him trapped him in a sticky impasse. Eventually, he made a choice and moved out of the home he shared with his wife and into a flat on his own. His girlfriend, the affair, was furious. His wife would send him emails pleading with him to reconsider. For someone who wasn't supposed to have an impact on anyone, this was a disaster, but it wasn't the first time he'd failed everyone by trying to hide the truth.

Keeping it all inside

Idris had been brought up to hide the truth when things went wrong or relationships failed. Things had gone wrong many times over the years but each time he had buried his feelings and used drinking, gambling and promiscuity to distract him from his unhappiness. Once he started telling me his story he didn't stop. He told me about everything he'd been dealing with, or not dealing with, and how eventually he'd started to contemplate suicide. The following week he cancelled his session and told me there was a work emergency. I didn't know if he'd ever come back, but I was pleased when he did and we were able to talk about why he'd cancelled – not for the reason he'd given, but because he felt guilty for offloading on me. According to his rules, he'd unfairly burdened me, sabotaged our relationship before it had even begun and caused me great distress. It told me something about the messages he'd received growing up. I asked him what he thought I might have said if he'd come to last week's session as planned.

'That's easy,' he said. 'You'd have said: "How could you, Idris! You really worried me! You ruined my week!" And you'd have given me a really stern look … like this.' He scowled at me.

The reaction he'd imagined from me was the reaction he would have got from his parents.

Idris told me that his parents were great and that he and his brothers had been happy growing up. He also told me that 'they weren't big believers in mental health' and that they didn't talk about how they felt. When he was young, he told me, he was known as 'a bit of a crier'. That wasn't acceptable in his family and he'd learned not to show anyone his tears. This was the code in Idris's house. You could be cheeky or playful, and you could misbehave, but you couldn't be upset – and above all, 'you mustn't worry your mother'. If he had ever felt tearful or looked anxious, his dad would look sternly at him, tell him off for upsetting her, and so he'd stopped. He stopped *showing* he was upset but that didn't mean he stopped feeling it. When his marriage was on the rocks, he didn't show anyone how much he was struggling. When his business was failing and he thought he might lose the house, he kept it all to himself. When he felt crippled by anxiety and depression, he would drink his feelings down. He didn't want to worry his parents. He didn't want to worry his friends. He didn't even want to worry me.

Fear of failure

Something shifted in Idris, his shoulders relaxed a little and he sat back in his chair as he acknowledged his fear of worrying people. We talked about what life had been like when he was growing up and he told me about the scrapes he'd got into, smiling fondly at the memories. Once, he recounted, he'd snuck a girl into his bedroom after his parents had gone to bed. He thought he'd got away with it but early the next morning, his mother had knocked loudly and stuck her head round the door, eyes screwed shut.

"'Good morning, dear,'" he put his hand over his eyes and affected his mother's high-pitched tone of disapproval, "'Does your friend take milk and sugar in her tea?'" He'd chuckled at this, remembering her reaction and how he and his brother would make merry mischief as teenagers, affable scamps, 'just boys being boys' according to his dad, and he'd ruffle their hair affectionately.

Idris liked this version of himself, the loveable rogue who sailed close to the wind but could be people's champion at the same time. That's why people liked him. He'd hide his sadness behind a few pints at the pub, talk about football with his mates and crack a few gags, never letting them see how broken he felt.

Idris was a Pacifier and felt shame if he ever upset anyone with his feelings. Vulnerability was tantamount to failure in his family and it terrified him. When his parents had been worried about him, they would scold him and withdraw. They would dismiss his feelings, tell him to be strong and to get on with it. That's what he saw his dad do in times of difficulty. If that failed, they would tell him to go to his room and come back down when he felt better. In reality, they hadn't known how to deal with their own feelings, so they had to avoid them and encourage him to avoid his. They were an endless source of practical support but they couldn't hold a space for him to feel in, they couldn't normalise his experiences growing up and encourage him to seek help when he needed it. Without help and without the ability to feel, Idris had trapped his pain inside and reached for ever more destructive ways to distract himself, for fear of revealing it to someone else and losing their relationship.

These destructive behaviours were somehow more acceptable in his model for being a man than expressing grief for the breakdown of his family. Gambling and promiscuity, over-working and drinking, were all more acceptable to his friends and peers than the vulnerability that he hid through these behaviours. When he did ultimately destroy a relationship, he took it as another stick to beat himself with and another failure, another reason to feel ashamed and another reason to hide his true feelings.

Idris came to understand that the way he thought about his emotions and behaviours was driven by his idea of what it meant to be male in his environment. He was missing the permission to feel, to ask for help and to have an impact on other people. It wasn't his feelings that had cost him his marriage, it was the reckless and selfish ways he'd behaved in his efforts to hide the truth.

On being male

Take a moment to think about the men in your household.

What did being male mean in your family?

Ask yourself what code you follow and where it came from. Perhaps you picked up from your parents that to be a boy meant being practical and non-emotional. Maybe your school or your friends reinforced it. Maybe your workplace echoes it now by rewarding being challenging and competitive, whilst discouraging sensitivity or reflection.

What did you see your male role models do in times of difficulty?

See if you can remember what the males in your family did and how they behaved in times of trouble.

My clients often report never seeing their father cry or, if on occasion they did, how uncomfortable it felt for them to witness and how out of character this seemed. Idris remembered his grandmother dying, on his father's side, and how the funeral was filled with restrained men, jaws clenched and eyes dry. He told me that things were starting to change for men now. He said his company was starting to take mental health more seriously and offer more emotional support. He said he'd even found that mental health would come up as a topic of discussion among his friends at the pub. 'Well, we talk about what we *think* about mental health,' he said with a knowing smile. 'I can't say we talk about how we *feel* about it yet.'

Shame and hiding

We all want to feel accepted. It's a prerequisite for the social animals that we are and the greatest threat to acceptance is shame. For a lot of men, to talk about how you feel or to express your vulnerability is comparable to weakness and still carries stigma. Shame is one of our most primal feelings, designed to keep us on the right side of the line or on the inside of the pack. To justify real shame, we must have done something terrible, something that would get us exiled from a just society. If someone slips up at work, makes a faux pas in a social situation, drives an inferior car, or bursts into tears, they can feel a sensation they might call shame. But none of these constitute shameful acts, none warrant a shame-filled response. So beholden are we to feeling socially acceptable that anything grazing the periphery of 'normal' starts to look atypical enough that we risk being banished to a social wilderness for a single wrong step.

You might recognise the feeling of shame. Perhaps you can re-examine it and notice that there was no shameful act to justify it. Perhaps you can spot that it doesn't even belong to you and it's really an inter-generational hangover that was passed down to you, inappropriate for the present day. If our parents were caught in their own shame, we can continue to collect shameful feelings that weren't ever ours. Their beliefs set according to their own parents' code of fear and shame around the social transgressions of *their* time are to be understood but laid to rest.

Shame is designed to drive us into hiding and to repress unacceptable desires; that was its function in the beginning, to motivate us to keep an ill-advised urge at bay in order not to risk rejection by society. That's still its safety function now but it's important to assess whether or not it's warranted or relevant today. If we don't discriminate between minor misdemeanours and grave transgressions of morality, we will feel shame where it doesn't belong and our reflex will be to hide. It's the hiding that causes the problems. If we believe vulnerability is shameful, we will bury it. If we believe one mistake means game over, we'll deny it. Vulnerability and mistakes are human, and Idris could have sought help for his problems at work and in his marriage if he'd been taught that it was OK to do so. Instead he had to hide, and the more we hide, the more ashamed we feel. It's a lonely downward spiral, one that's hard to interrupt on your own, and by the time I see men like Idris, they have often behaved in exactly the ways that would get them rejected in the end. The tragedy is that the affairs and the gambling and the addictions were merely the side effects of misplaced shame attached to vulnerability, that had driven them underground in the first place.

Perhaps, like Idris, shame makes you hide parts of yourself, even when your crimes are only natural feelings or normal thoughts, or simply mistakes that you've made along the way. If you can interrupt that cycle of hiding, you can begin to test your assumptions and find out what happens when you reveal the truth. You can share your 'shadow side' and find out that you are already loveable and acceptable, that you can please yourself and still be in the pack. Having a shadow side isn't shameful, it's human, but hiding it might lead you to act out in shameful ways that result in the very rejection you were so desperate to avoid.

Shame and the people-pleaser

For people-pleasers, shame was often the stick employed by fearful parents to stop children behaving in ways that they couldn't cope with, or that presented them with feelings they couldn't resolve. For Idris growing up, the social code for men in his pack was: 'Don't show your feelings.' Labelling him a 'crier' triggered early feelings of shame that made him stop his tears. Telling him that his feelings upset his mother was another reason for him to stop. As an adult, he still feared the rejection of the pack so he'd continued to follow the old code, even when he was drowning in his distress. We need our feelings to help us grieve, to help us evolve, to stand up for ourselves and to help us let go. Without his feelings, Idris couldn't resolve the challenges life threw at him and he couldn't reach out for support. He tried to outrun his feelings but they kept catching up with him, driving him down one self-destructive escape route after another. More loss, more feelings, more shame and more hiding.

Men like Idris can be easily misunderstood in our society. Judged on their behaviour alone, they can seem a bit too good at pleasing themselves already – the egotistical philanderer living a hedonistic life and thinking only of himself – but if we also take into account their motivations, we can get another perspective. Pleasing yourself doesn't mean caring *only* about yourself, it means caring *enough* about yourself to do the right thing and risk being disliked for it, in order to make intimate, authentic, sustaining relationships. Idris wasn't contemplating suicide because he lived a life of carefree self-gratification, he wanted to die because he felt desperate and alone. Caring *enough* about himself would look like risking the dislike of his family and friends to break the rules of his male code and acknowledge his feelings. Pleasing himself would look like asking for help, not as a sign of weakness but as a sign of strength.

Permission to feel

Idris came to therapy and got permission to feel and to ask for help, but he had to reach breaking point to get there. Maybe you need permission to feel too. To stop being strong and stoic and to ask for help, before you get to breaking point yourself. Maybe you can recognise your parents' blind spots too, the social code they were following from their own parents. Give yourself permission to interrupt them now and to challenge their usefulness to you today.

Brains change and cognitions are wired according to the cultural inputs we receive and the responses we make. There are differences between male and female brains but these are largely not the anatomical or cognitive differences of our design, they are the product of our cultural references; we are primarily cultural beings, after all. When boys are told to 'man up' we create an input that tells them they can't be vulnerable, they can't struggle and they mustn't feel. When we tell them 'nice guys finish last' we teach them they must be pushy if they want to win.

Perhaps you can look around at boys growing up now and notice that they deserve a different code. One that makes space for them to share their feelings, without judgment or shame. The code of a patriarchy affords men power, but power alone doesn't stand us in such good stead when life gives us lemons. An exoskeleton of power can be torn away and leave us helpless in the face of crisis or grief. If our only recourse is to fight back in defence, we'll wage a war between us and others, or between conflicted parts of ourselves. Our feelings corrode us from the inside until we career towards collapse: the mid-life crisis, the burnout, the suicidal thoughts. When life happens, power won't be as useful as the ability to self-regulate, to ask for help and tune in to our feelings for the important data they contain.

'Don't feel' is not an exclusively male domain – it affects men and women – but in my experience it resides unconsciously in men more often. Men and women can reach for equality more meaningfully if we recognise that 'privilege' is not one-dimensional. Historically, the patriarchy has bred patriarchs – powerful males not encumbered by vulnerability or sensitivity or empathy. Ruthless towards others *and* towards themselves. Not an advantage to the men or women overpowered by them and not an advantage to themselves, when faced with failure or loss. In this way, a traditionally male message of head without heart and thinking without feeling, disadvantages us all as it advances a limited ideology of competition and individualism at the cost of the intimate and the communal.

If we raise boys (and girls) who can feel for themselves, they will have the capacity to feel for others and to relate with empathy and compassion. If we raise girls (and boys) to own their power and assert themselves, to have needs and potency, they will be protected by self-worth. If we deny our needs or have no sense of agency, we leave our safety in the hands of people we'll need to please, even when they don't have our best interests at heart. To be truly and usefully equal, we need permission to be both vulnerable *and* empowered.

The perfect gentleman

One stereotypical male pleasing persona is the 'perfect gentleman', someone who was brought up to say 'ladies first' and 'after you'. Romcoms have taught us to expect men to give us their coat, buy us flowers or flag down our taxi, if he's a true gent he might even watch the romcom with us. But it doesn't leave much room for them to be 'real' men – by which I don't mean tough and manly, I mean imperfect with emotional needs of their own.

Matt

Matt was a Shadow pleaser but not a great one, as it turned out, because he couldn't keep it up for long. When he found himself alone, he'd go to the pub and buy a round; when he felt insecure, he'd flood someone else with compliments. He'd love-bomb relative strangers with his attention and generosity and take pride in refusing their offers of reciprocation. But he couldn't see it through and inevitably he'd come to resent the people who had accepted his love on such selfish, one-way terms.

He was good at his job as a charity fundraiser, charming his way into the pockets of rich companies and heading up a department of adoring disciples. Romantically it was a less successful story, and he often found himself in disappointing one-night stands, complicated workplace relationships, or flings with married women. He was a serial first-dater and had a talent for it. The hour or two of witty and engaging conversation came easily to him and didn't risk revealing any of his other, less-forgiving features. He could be the happy-go-lucky cheeky chappy, fun and gregarious, interested and thoughtful. He'd sweep them off their feet for an evening, exchanging numbers and promises at the end of the night, but he'd never call them because there was no way he could keep up the act for a second date.

Matt's raison d'être was to make people happy, primarily women. His mother had been heartbroken when his father left and he'd looked after her and his younger sisters as best he could, always trying to make them smile and laugh. He was only twelve but she'd tell him he was 'the man of the house' and her 'knight in shining armour' and he'd do his best to measure up.

He had a reputation for being a gentleman among everyone who knew him, always holding doors open, giving up seats and carrying bags. He'd insist on paying when the bill came, he'd take his nieces shopping for prom dresses and feed his next-door neighbour's cat when she went away. If women were happy, he felt happy. He felt good about himself and on a deeper level, he felt secure in being their hero, the gentleman he had been brought up to be. The feeling of security was always short-lived, however. He knew it wasn't genuine when he pleased people, or at least it wasn't the full story. After his neighbour came home, he'd feel angry if she didn't invite him in for a drink. After he took his nieces shopping, he'd feel rejected when they made plans to see their friends the following weekend.

Be careful what you wish for

'Be careful how you advertise yourself,' I warned him one day. Matt was in the business of making people happy and he advertised his services with a slogan that might as well have said 'If you're happy, then I'm happy'. The people that took up his offer expected him to please them willingly, that's what the sign said after all, and they were confused when the supply dried up or they were landed with a big emotional bill. Matt attracted friendships and relationships with the promise of limitless one-way attention and gratification. He led with his chivalry and flattery and deployed his best behaviour to buy their company for a time, but ultimately he'd resent them for not seeing behind the facade and eventually he'd turn on them, withdrawing his affection. When he stopped pleasing them they'd be surprised and disappointed (understandably so), reinforcing his belief that only his people-pleasing version was acceptable. Once they weren't happy, Matt couldn't be happy, and he'd move on to love-bomb someone else.

Realistically, Matt's authentic slogan might as well have said 'If you're not happy, then I *can't* be happy' but that might have attracted fewer customers.

How do you advertise yourself?

What does your slogan say about you?

What do you unconsciously offer? How do you promise to please people? Think about the genuine type of relationship you want to offer and be yourself, not a

granter of wishes. What do you want to offer that takes
into account your own needs as well as someone else's?
If we can risk attracting people with who we really are,
without the facade, we might find that we get fewer knocks
on the door but the ones that knock will be the right ones,
the ones who are secure enough to meet their own needs
and can be alongside us in meeting ours. Rewrite your
Please Yourself slogan and be proud of the offer you make.

Idris and Matt both tried to be who they believed people wanted
them to be, in order to meet their needs and feel part of the
pack. If we never felt the protection of the pack as a child, we
might have learned to live without it and find other ways to stay
safe. If our feelings were never important, we might defend
ourselves by deciding that we don't care. In many of the male
clients I work with, this is where I see the emergence of the
Resistor.

A cautionary tale

A familiar figure arriving in my therapy room is the man reeling from the shock of divorce.

It's not an uncommon story: this is a man who has worked
hard for years, paying the bills at home and managing upwards
at work, often from a background where he also felt
responsibility from a young age. He survives the pressures to
perform by resisting the emotional responsibility for the
relationships in his life. Seeking to get away from duties at
home, he craves freedom and independence, believing that to
take care of himself would feel infinitely easier than taking care
of everyone else.

In one couple I worked with, this was the man who would complain about having to 'babysit' when his wife went out for an evening, even though it was his own children he was taking care of. If she suggested he take them to the park at the weekend, he'd respond as though it were an imposition, muttering, 'Daddy day-care again,' under his breath. His friendship pack honoured the same Resistor code. The comrades he met at the pub would share war stories of being henpecked by their wives, while they watched sport on the big screen and ordered one more for the road. Brothers in arms, they'd comfort each other when they finally had to drink up and 'get back to the missus'. Eventually, his wife grew tired of feeling like his prison warden, forever asking him to take an interest in his children or spend time with her and getting only an eye-roll in reply, and she called time on the relationship.

These are the men who thought they wanted freedom and independence when, in reality, they only wanted these as a reaction to having felt unimportant in the past. They trained themselves out of wanting to feel close because it was never available and their genuine relationship needs were replaced by the assumed indifference of the Resistor. Their wives don't want to control them and don't want to be cast as the villains, nor do they want to be with someone who only spends time with the family under duress. Resistors can sound like they don't care what people think – they don't suffer fools gladly or pander to the pressure to people-please, but they can create a protective persona of indifference or belligerence and miss the grain of truth within the feedback. They isolate themselves from others and can make themselves unloveable to avoid feeling unloved. They believe themselves to be safely outside the clutches of people-pleasing but are firmly in the grip of the original male code, as they forego emotional intimacy to be 'one of the lads'.

These are the lone wolves, seeking independence in response to the lack of any known alternative or co-dependency in the past. If they can learn to communicate how they feel and what they need, they can find both freedom and belonging *within* their relationship; they can please themselves within their family. If they can't, then they find themselves achieving the liberation they thought they always wanted but in a way that loses them their family for good.

Making intimate relationships

Males often gravitate towards hierarchies from an early age; perhaps for biological reasons, perhaps based on the hierarchies they observed within their families – nature or nurture or both. Guys can use the inbuilt benchmarks of sport to compete or belong, they can compare the engines in their cars or climb the ladder at work. Hierarchies readily create people-pleasers as their members respond either by following orders or fighting back, instead of self-pleasing appropriately. Their focus can be on progress and status at the cost of intimacy and relationship, and a win at work can mitigate a loss at home. Personal relationships can suffer as they focus on impressing their boss, and partners often recount the exasperation they feel when their boyfriends or husbands seem to save their best selves for work.

For many males, where there is competition, there is a reason to perform. At home there may be no competition – no league table or promotion or pay rise – so performance can feel unnecessary. Once a relationship has been secured and a goal has been achieved, it can be easy to disengage and reserve your energy for some other competition, somewhere else. In fact, disengaging at home can be actively encouraged by a male code; it can even become another domain for competition, with men shaming each other for being 'under the thumb'. To observe this male code, you must grumble about the 'ball and chain' and you must not outgrow your pack, even if you would welcome a meaningful grown-up existence with the support of a romantic partner.

Our relationships are designed to develop through stages. We begin with a handshake and a hello, we make small talk and we structure our time together through shared activities and common interests. Many relationships plateau at this point but can still be fulfilling friendships. However, if we want to build deeper links, we must go beyond pastimes and joint pursuits to a connection of intimacy, complete with the authenticity and engagement therein. When the traditional male code limits its followers to only feeling-free connections, it's no wonder that male conversation will default to sport, or technology or cars, safe in an arena of structured activities. Anyone who challenges the code by expressing vulnerability or reaching for intimacy can look like a dangerous outlier and be told to 'grow a pair' – their peers gently guiding them back within the norms of the group using a generous dose of shame.

If you were taught that vulnerability is a sign of weakness, you may have learned to hide your feelings and rely more on casual friendships to sustain you now. You might not even know that you do it but maybe you're aware at times that there is something missing from your relationships, or that something gets in the way of you making authentic connections. Many of the men I work with report feeling lonely in their lives, in a way that women don't. Men can miss the support network that comes through a lifetime of sharing and expression, but only realise when the shit hits the fan, and they find they can't just bounce back or problem-solve the situation. Maybe you notice that your friendships work well when times are good and conversation is light but they aren't a natural source of emotional comfort to you when things get tough or you need help. If so, there might be a case to invest in some connections that have the potential for intimacy, even if that calls for some vulnerability on your part. Who knows, whoever you reach out to may be in need of something similar themselves.

Vulnerability doesn't make you unloveable, no matter what you were taught in the beginning, but your defences might. Remember that the shame was never yours in the first place; it was the relic of a fearful past and archaic attitudes towards masculinity. Behind your walls, nobody can hurt you – but nobody can love you either. Bring down the walls and let someone in. It's your right to tell them how you feel. It's their privilege to listen.

As you become better able to please yourself, you'll be in a position to share what you've learned with others who might need to make a similar journey – as we'll see in the next chapter, when we explore how it feels to be on the receiving end of people-pleasing.

Being People-pleased

There's an exercise I sometimes use in couples' counselling to explore the people-pleasing dynamics within a relationship. I give the couple a single sheet of paper to hold between them, and I ask them to negotiate so that only one person is left holding it in the end.

The results are always interesting. Of course there is no one way, no right approach, but it serves to bring their unconscious assumptions and behaviours out into the open and that's where we get to talk about them.

Elton and Andrea were one of these couples. They had come to therapy because Andrea felt their relationship was stuck in a rut. Their daughter had recently flown the nest and the freedom and excitement that Andrea had fantasised about had been replaced with a reality of boredom and frustration. She'd found herself thinking about calling it a day because, whilst she still loved Elton, she couldn't bear to grow old with someone who seemed satisfied to forever be a 'passenger' in life.

I gave them the piece of paper and explained the exercise. What happened next didn't come as much of a surprise.

ELTON: 'You have it, darling.'

ANDREA: 'I don't think that's the point of the exercise. I
think we're supposed to talk about it and understand
more about the way we behave.'

ELTON: 'Oh OK, yes, OK. I'll take it then.'

ANDREA: 'You're not getting it! We're supposed to talk
about it!'

ELTON: 'Sorry, sorry, sorry … What shall we talk about?'

ANDREA: 'What do YOU want to talk about? Why can't
you take the lead? Why do you always look to me to
tell you what to think or what to do? This is exactly
what I'm talking about!'

ELTON: 'Shit. Sorry. I've done it again, haven't I? OK, let's
see, hmmm …'

ANDREA: [*Sighs and lets go of paper*]

ELTON: [*Puts paper down on table and looks to me*] 'Sorry.'

The problem with being 'pleased'

As Andrea knew all too well, it can be draining to be on the
receiving end of a people-pleaser. Scared of disappointing you,
they leave you with the burden of making every decision, and
coast in the slipstream of your energy and initiative. They bring
nothing to the table for fear that what they bring might be
wrong. They shy away from conflict to the extent that they
extinguish any passion. They've already said sorry before you
can open your mouth.

People-pleasers can be really irritating in relationships. Of
course, sometimes it can feel nice to be around someone who
appears to be considerate and generous, flexible and unassum-
ing. But most of the time there is an unconscious trade-off

being made. If you are the recipient, you must accept their pleasing ways, and reassure them that they have been suitably selfless, praise them for their subservience and be grateful for their dedication. Andrea was sick and tired of it. What had begun as Elton's harmless people-pleasing now felt like a drain on her life force, and he became spineless and desperate in his need to keep her close. In their example, Elton's need to please had worsened since their daughter had left home. He felt purposeless without his role as dad and insecure at the idea that Andrea no longer had this as a cast-iron reason to stay with him. But his frantic lunges for her approval were driving her away, and his attempts to be easy-going were only serving to inflame her irritation.

Perhaps you know an annoying people-pleaser. You make a plan to go to the cinema but when it comes to choosing the film, they insist that you decide. Even when you remind them that it's their turn, they twitch uncomfortably and try to second-guess the film they think you might prefer. Uncomfortable with the weight of a possible wrong decision and grateful that you're there at all, they thrust their card at the cashier and pay for your ticket before you have a chance to argue. 'My treat!' they sing, to make themselves feel better.

If a people-pleaser can be honest with themselves, they'll come to recognise that they don't do it for someone else, they do it to remedy their own insecurity. It's ultimately a selfish act wrapped up in a selfless bow and that's a surefire way to piss people off in the end.

Realising that people-pleasing doesn't actually please people can help us take permission to stop doing it ourselves. At best it can be irritating but at worst it's disrespectful and duplicitous, if we use it to manoeuvre the other person into a position we feel comfortable with. If we can acknowledge its toxicity, we can take steps to start pleasing ourselves and stop damaging the very relationships we were trying to preserve. Andrea wanted Elton to care enough about her that he would find the courage to have the difficult discussions that are part of any intimate relationship. She wanted him to share the load of real life and be authentic, even when it felt scary for him. She wanted him to be emotionally available to her and to offer a more meaningful and securing connection. That's what Elton wanted too; he just didn't know there was another way to do it.

Helping people-pleasers to stop pleasing often involves an uncomfortable process of bringing their attention to the unconscious undercurrents they create. It's not the people-pleaser's actions that are the problem, necessarily – although these tend to be fairly hit-and-miss, restricted to the narrow repertoire of what they believe to be pleasing rather than what the individual might actually appreciate. The bigger problem lies in their ulterior motives. Like Elton, people-pleasers need their recipient to react positively to get the sense of acceptance and reassurance they crave, and it creates an imbalance that is not conducive to an adult-to-adult relationship. Like Andrea, the recipient of the people-pleasing may not want to hold all the power, but they are landed with the responsibility for it regardless.

It's not a conscious process but it must be brought into consciousness to be reset. The people-pleaser needs to own their experience and recognise their process, in order to reclaim their power and liberate the one on the receiving end from the responsibility of bearing it for them.

Your experience as someone who has fallen foul of pleasing pressures in the past will help you understand when someone else is acting under the same forces and, if you also know what it's like to be on the receiving end of a people-pleaser, you're in an ideal position to share the reality of being pleased. If you have a relationship that was previously based on pleasing and being pleased, you can start to help each other to negotiate honestly about what you both need, on your own paths towards pleasing yourselves. Instead of accepting each other's outdated people-pleasing efforts, you can help each other work towards a more up-to-date, respectful and accepting relationship that meets both your authentic needs today. If there is a friend or a colleague who you think would be up for a more up-to-date and honest connection, who would welcome a different approach whereby you free each other of the burden of pleasing and being pleased, you could make this new contract with them. You could say: 'How about we make a deal where you tell me if there's something that's not working for you and I tell you if there's something not working for me, and we try to fix it together?'

As you stop pleasing them, and stop accepting their pleasing of you, you build a relationship of authenticity and you can learn to be yourselves, together.

Unconditional acceptance

I am often on the receiving end of people trying to please me in the therapy room. It might be the client who tries to tip me after a session in which they feel they've been particularly 'hard work', or the one who brings me a cup of coffee because they'd feel too rude to drink theirs alone, or the one who stands outside in the pouring rain because they'd feel too awkward to push the doorbell a minute or two before our appointment time. I can generally tell on day one when a client will want me to like them, to approve of them or to validate them. For these clients, it can be a painful process as I gently invite them to explore what it would be like if I *didn't* like them and I *didn't* approve. Kindly but firmly taking away a trusted comfort blanket of people-pleasing so that their own thoughts and feelings can fill the space and they can outgrow their childlike compliance, to learn about who they are and find themselves equally and unconditionally acceptable to me and to themselves.

When we realise the language of compliance and good behaviour can't cut it in the therapy room, we get the opportunity to communicate in new ways, to feel understood more deeply and validated more completely, for who we are, not who we believe we should be.

Therapy is one example of a relationship that can offer this equanimity and compassion. In therapy, a client gets an opportunity to forego their people-pleasing patterns and be seen for who they really are in the hope that, if they can feel accepted in the therapy room, they can risk it in the real world.

You could take these learnings and apply them to your own relationships, to reset them with mutual permission, to please yourselves and break the chains of people-pleasing. You can give yourself permission to stop your own pleasing behaviours and take comfort from the fact that interrupting someone else's pleasing efforts might actually help them too, leaving you free to reconnect on a new level of authenticity.

Whether we're in therapy or not, we can help each other to make this journey, if we are willing to create a space in our everyday relationships that is authentic and non-judgmental. Unconditional acceptance is the star for all recovering people-pleasers to sail by, a direction of travel which can lead them to the self-esteem and freedom they need to please themselves.

Stress and depression

For us to be healthy, we need to have the ability and permission to respond to our emotions, but people-pleasers are often working without either. Human beings are designed to be able to experience times of stress and to survive, all mammals are, but if we were wild animals being chased by a predator, we'd only have to live off our emergency responses for a minute or so. By then we would either have got away, or we'd be dead. Say we did get away, then our next task would be to get to safety, underneath a tree tucked away somewhere secluded, and there we might begin to shake. Our bodies would process the trauma we had just experienced, releasing the chemicals we had produced in our natural fight or flight response. Humans have found ways to override this natural response and, far from the single minute of stress we are designed to fire off and then regulate, we have found ways to live with moderate or even high levels of chronic stress for long periods of time, sometimes even for lifetimes, carrying anxiety as our permanent baseline. We never process our stress, we live on our nerves and we try to people-please our way to safety.

In a similar vein, we can recognise that depression is not the same as feeling down. It would be truer to say it's not feeling *at all*. It's the unconscious act of depressing all feelings until they leave a flat and barren wasteland where joy and motivation once resided. Depression is often a result of the unconscious suppression of grief or anger or fear, feelings that might threaten to topple a people-pleaser if they were to give them their full attention. Feelings that risk them becoming unable to function or relate in the ways they think they should, thus failing their people-pleasing conditions and seeing them rejected by those they need to please.

For a people-pleaser, paying attention to your own feelings is not the norm. It's your role to pay attention to the feelings of other people, to keep *them* happy and take away *their* pain. If you're lucky, your people-pleasing efforts will be rewarded by their positive reaction to you and, at least for a time, you might take a feeling of OK-ness from that. When a pleaser fails to be pleasing enough, or faces a challenge or need of their own, their original programming to prioritise other people prevents them from asking for help, and anxiety and depression can result.

Storytelling to process stress

When someone arrives at therapy, anxious or depressed or both, the first task is to help them tell their story, to do that piece of processing that a wild animal might do through trembling. Humans have language and with it the ability to integrate their thoughts and feelings through storytelling. It allows them to bring forward their thoughts and feelings, however desperate or ridiculous or unacceptable they might seem to them, to enable their bodies and minds to reclaim their experiences and to bear witness to their reality. They can stitch together the parts they find too frightening or shameful or hopeless, into a tapestry that begins to make sense and reveal their humanity and needs. Only then can they tune in to what is wrong and redesign a liberated life where anxiety and depression no longer keep them frozen in their tracks. They can be free to feel and able to respond, aware of the reactions of others as products of their own conditioning. To be authentic, likeable or dislikeable, and OK either way: this is real resilience.

So often clients fear being disliked if their loved ones should discover the truth, if they should know how dark their thoughts are or how paranoid they have become. They predict reactions in which they are alienated as a family reject or some onerous burden to bear. They come to therapy precisely because it's the therapist's job to listen and *not* judge, to have no skin in the game and to be unbiased and unconditional in their regard. When a client says to me, 'It sounds ridiculous,' or 'This will sound really mean,' I make sure they hear me say: 'It won't to me.' And it won't. There is nothing I haven't heard over years of working with individuals, couples, families and organisations. No thought too dark, no feeling too unpalatable. These aren't the dislikeable, unacceptable forays into impropriety, these are what it is to be human, and to be human is complicated.

Anya

Anya came *to* therapy but was never *in* therapy, dutifully attending our appointments in body but emotionally buried under the weight of her depression.

She was a considerate, cautious, gentle young woman, a writer by trade. I understood her struggle but, at times, found her company to be draining and effortful. In her attempts to be pleasing in therapy, she would adopt a position of subservience to me. She'd try to Classic please me by writing me short stories and bringing me books. She would sit in near silence for fifty minutes without making eye contact and then email me an apology afterwards, for failing me, or upsetting me, or for not answering my questions honestly enough. She'd do the same to her girlfriend and, for fear of upsetting her, Anya would hide behind a wall, making it impossible for her girlfriend to reach her.

She was afraid that if she said or did the wrong thing in our sessions, I would tell her we couldn't work together any more. Paralysed by her Pacifier patterns, she feared rejection and would keep her feelings and darkness to herself and then feel scared that I would think she had wasted my time.

She was the client I'd discuss in my clinical supervision more than any other at that time. My reactions to her weren't simply my own feelings of frustration, they were feelings transferred onto me as a reflection of the way she organised the whole world to react. She'd try so hard to not displease anyone that she frustrated everyone with her blocks and her defences. She tried to hide her painful feelings for fear of losing those she cared for, but her resulting depression created the greater divide.

It was easy to understand from the fragments of the history that she shared why she would be so afraid of rejection, and her early memories were hard to hear. Once, she told me, she'd broken a glass or spilt something (she couldn't remember which, because she was only three or four) and her parents responded by packing her belongings in a little suitcase and depositing them, and her, outside on the doorstep. She remembered sitting next to her suitcase, understanding that she wasn't allowed to live there any more but not knowing what to do. Eventually her parents opened the door and let her come back in. 'They wanted to teach me a lesson,' she said, numbly. There were many examples like this, times in which her parents had made her feel terrified that any wrong move could see her sent away. It was heartbreaking to listen to and yet, counter-intuitively, my role had to be more than just a reassuring voice of nurture now. She'd had plenty of those over the years but they just set her up to feel beholden, grateful for the compassion at the time but all the more fearful of losing it again should she ever make a mistake. My acceptance of her had to be unconditional, which meant I would never disapprove of her as her parents had but I couldn't give her my approval either, she needed to be free of the weight of my approval altogether to look inside for her own. It took time and we had to help her feel secure enough to emotionally emerge at all, before we could even contemplate the prospect of rejection. One day, she brought in a carefully crafted poem that she'd written about me. It was undoubtedly beautiful. It felt like a cat depositing a mouse at its owner's feet, searching in earnest for praise and validation, and we used it to bring her attention to the relationship between us. 'What would it be like,' I began, 'if I was pleased with you ... if I appreciated your gift ... if I felt that you were working hard here?'

She looked at me suspiciously. 'Well ... it would feel good, I guess?'

I continued gently, 'So then ... what if I didn't? What if I wasn't pleased with you or I didn't want your gift ... how would that be?' She cowered as she experienced the possibility that she hadn't pleased me and couldn't please me, that she couldn't earn her place and was powerless once again, left sitting on the doorstep. We explored what it would be like for her to put down her pleasing patterns when she came to therapy, to take a brief reprieve from the code she followed in the rest of her life, to be pleasing, silent and submissive. We worked together to understand what it would be like to feel accepted by me, for who she was, not for what she did or didn't do, and with this understanding we brought in the possibility for change.

Our work began anew after this, more authentically and more meaningfully. Anya was afraid that her girlfriend would abandon her if she displeased her, but trying to manage her girlfriend's feelings had left Anya ill-equipped to take care of her own and the depression that had formed in their place was the far greater threat to their relationship. Anya came to therapy to learn how to please herself and practised releasing herself from feeling responsible for her girlfriend's feelings, by releasing herself from feeling responsible for mine.

You're welcome

Let's take a moment to hear from the part of you that you keep hidden from others, the part of you that you believe to be unacceptable.

What is the worst thing someone could know about you?

Perhaps there is a feeling or a thought or an urge that you rule out as shameful or mean or ridiculous.

The same rule applies, whether you go to therapy or not. Nothing you think or feel is unacceptable, it is all part of being human and all of you is welcome. Let yourself tell your own story, if only to yourself at first. It might help you to get behind those initial defences of fear or guilt and find out what it is you truly feel and what you really need.

And, if you choose to help someone else who is caught in a pattern of people-pleasing, you might offer them this same acceptance, to listen to their story for its meaning, with curiosity not judgment.

Withholding praise

When I work with pleasing clients, it's important to let them know that they *can't* please me. Not because their efforts aren't pleasing enough, but because it's not a currency I accept. You are OK by me whatever you do and however you are. I might ask you to get curious about why you do what you do, I might confront the discounts you make or the narrative you tell yourself. I might block your attempts to organise my reactions, not because I disapprove but because it's my job to help you have your *own* reactions and to hear yourself clearly, without censorship or adaptation and without running your story through a filter of social acceptability.

I have to take care in my practice not to over-adapt to my pleasing clients. If I did, I could unwittingly collude with their struggle and join them in each of us taking responsibility for the other. When I scheduled an increase in fees, it triggered an important process for one of my long-term clients, Lars.

Lars

Lars was a 'good' client. A Classic pleaser, he was always on time and always understanding if I was ill or had to cancel. He waited patiently for me to return to work after my maternity leave. When I moved away, he would take two trains to reach me, continuing to attend every week, fully engaged in his therapeutic journey.

When it came time for me to increase my fees, I gave my contractual notice and advised each of my clients individually. Lars came to therapy the next week and was visibly agitated. After fifteen minutes of hearing about his irritation with his boss and the ways in which his neighbour had annoyed him, I asked:

'Perhaps you're angry with me too?'

His reaction was one first of panic and then relief.

'I'm fuming!' he said eventually, with fire in his eyes.

He went on, 'I've spent all this time and money on therapy! I never cancel, I never mess you around and yet you treat me like this – it's never enough, you want more, it's greedy. You're just the same as the rest of them – take, take, take.'

I let him finish. He took a deep breath and swallowed back tears.

He felt sad for the years he'd thanklessly over-worked for everyone else, only to be rewarded with higher expectations and greater demands. He was angry with himself for doing it and for allowing himself to be used by others, others who weren't even aware that they were using him, who believed him when he said that his gifts were freely given, and others like me who were never persuaded by his pleasing in the first place.

He had martyred himself in the hope that others would do the same for him. If he was a 'good' client, he hoped he would endear himself to me and I might reward him by being a 'good' therapist. One who would be kind and generous and would thank him for his efforts. He was an only child to a single-parent and his mother had been vulnerable in her own ways. Lars would describe how, growing up, his mother would often tell him he looked pale and keep him home from school: 'I think most of the time she was just lonely,' he told me. 'I think I was taking care of her more than she was taking care of me.'

All his life he had looked for a good enough 'parent', one who wouldn't take from him, one who wouldn't expect something in return and one who could care for him without strings attached, a secure, one-way supply of safety and support. For him, I had represented this potential but by directing his attention back to the professional nature of our relationship, I had burst his bubble and brought him back to reality. He was angry, but mostly he was sad that the gap had existed in the first place.

In reality, a 'good' therapist is one who is real and authentic, both supportive and challenging as the work demands. One who won't reward their clients for the maladaptive behaviours they have learned to deploy in the outside world, who won't reinforce the beliefs that they must meet set conditions in order to be judged worthy. One who won't fill the gap left by the generations before but will care enough to work through the feelings that it brings up for them now.

To do so, I believe a 'good' therapist must also know his or her own worth and model this to the clients they work with. I take care to follow the ethical guidelines of the regulatory body, to act in the client's interest and to not act in ways which are harmful to them. And yet, to do this I may in fact have to disturb their status quo in ways that feel confronting or challenging to them at times. I may have to increase my fees, or change my working practices or take time off. I can't please them or make up for their original parent but I can commit to bringing my whole self to the therapeutic relationship now and be available to work through past ruptures in the present, in a safe way that feels different and in which my client has new-found power and permission too. A 'good' friend, or partner, or employer might need to do the same. To model their ability to please themselves and reward self-pleasing in others.

Part of the reason my pleasing clients can trust that they can do no 'wrong' in my consulting room, is by also knowing that they can do no 'right'. There is no judgment, only the space and curiosity and compassion to find out what lies behind the people-pleasing. To be a 'good' client, you don't have to be likeable, you can tell me when I've missed your point or got something wrong and I can say sorry and make repair. To be a 'good' therapist I don't have to be likeable either. If I had rewarded Lars's pleasing behaviours with my own self-sacrifice I would have modelled to him that this was what was required of him also. I would have risked a repeat of that first model from his childhood, taught him to be good and patient and undemanding, and blindly hope that others would appreciate it.

We risk repeating early models in our personal relationships too. If we people-please those around us, we might communicate that this is also what we expect from them. If we accept their people-pleasing in return, we train them to continue putting our needs above their own. As a therapist, or a parent, or perhaps just as a human, we have a responsibility to model and not martyr. To lead by example and please yourself, and free them up to do the same.

I gave Lars an opportunity to be angry with me and for that to be OK. To explore the elements that were about the present but even more importantly, the elements that felt like a replay of the past. I could show him that he was just as acceptable to me, and just as welcome, in his anger as he was in his compliance. My acceptance of him was unconditional and he could stop trying to please me.

Shiny sides

Only when my clients can put away their shiny sides and find that they are still accepted by me, that I'm still willing to sit alongside them and understand why, can they get beyond the critical self-talk, the anxiety that keeps them on edge or the depression that keeps them hopeless. Only then can they hear their authentic feelings and understand what they need. Only then can they update the messages they were given about who they were to be in the world, how they were to behave, what their purpose was, in order to start living their own lives fully instead of living off the crumbs of the lives of others.

Prisons of praise

Praise isn't always what it's cracked up to be. It can train us into behaving in ways that others find acceptable or 'easy' and restrict our options to please ourselves.

What do people praise you for?

Perhaps you're often told that you're thoughtful or kind, or you have a reputation for being generous and supportive.

If your friends were going to describe your strengths, what might they say? On a good day, how would you describe yourself? Let's call this your 'shiny' side, the acceptable version, endorsed by others and introjected by you.

It's important not to over-accept your shiny side because it will push your shadow side further underground and further reinforce those restrictive conditions of worth. If we want to be free from our inner critic, we also have to give up the hit of praise that we get when we please people. If we don't want to feel like we're getting it wrong, we need to let go of the notion that we could be getting it right.

Likewise, it's important not to praise those we love for how they people-please for us.

What do you praise others for?

Over-accepting or praising their pleasing patterns will
reinforce that this is what you expect, even when it may
not be what you want, and it will keep them holding a pose
for you that they believe is integral to your relationship.

You could be brave and let them know that you don't
actually like it when they look to you for approval or run
their every decision past you. If they need your reassurance
or defer to you whenever you make arrangements, you can
tell them that it feels imbalanced or onerous. You could tell
them what you would like by way of a relationship and
see whether they're up for that. Free yourselves to please
yourselves and let your feedback be real so that your
relationship can be too.

This is the offer that therapists make: to be outside of the
people-pleasing patterns of their clients and to be someone
who can't be charmed or won over and so then can't be lost or
let down. It gives clients, often for the first time, an opportunity
to experiment with being who they really are and to find out
that they are already worthy, important and deserving of
respect, from other people and from themselves. It can be a first
experience, within the safety of a therapeutic microclimate, to
be tried on for size before taking into the outside world and
real-life relationships. If you try it on and find that it fits, you
can share it with the people who you notice get caught up
pleasing you.

The rings of relationships

You don't have to be in therapy to gather evidence that you are acceptable just as you are; you can experiment with pleasing yourself anywhere. Start in the domains that feel safest and build up the courage to tackle the relationships that matter most.

Imagine a set of concentric circles, and at the centre are those relationships that feel the most significant or perhaps most risky. For many of us, that will be our family of origin. In the ring around these might be your partner and your children – your family of today – still significant but perhaps less loaded with material from the past. Outside these might be a ring of friends, and then colleagues, neighbours and associates, until finally there will be a ring for the strangers in the street. Start your please-yourself journey on the outer ring if you feel at all unsure and work your way into the middle.

Let yourself be in that outer ring, in the supermarket for example, and practise making yourself important and of worth. Stand up for yourself if someone jumps the queue, allow yourself to take the last item on the shelf. Take your time when you pack your bags at the checkout and don't apologise if someone tuts. Give yourself permission to have an impact on other people and leave the responsibility for this impact with them. As you gather evidence that you can do this successfully in that outermost ring, that ancient part of your brain that scans for risk will store this as information for next time, and motivate you to act this way again. Let it bring you gently closer towards the centre circle, gathering evidence that you can be yourself, be important and be OK, with your associates, your neighbours and your colleagues. And let the evidence allow you to feel confident to show up as yourself with your friends, free to speak your mind and ready to negotiate.

If you meet rupture, as you undoubtedly will along the way, allow yourself to make repair. Say sorry if you've done something wrong, but not if someone else has wronged you. Remind yourself in those situations that anger is the appropriate alternative to guilt, felt and expressed in a grown-up way as energy for change and the restatement of a boundary, not as rage or retribution. As you find that you can use your feelings to protect yourself and point yourself towards the right repairs, you can bring the risk of rupture into your more intimate relationships. If we are willing to make repair then we can risk more honest relationships with our partners, until we might even find that we are ready to be our most authentic selves within our families of origin too.

Some clients can be real with their friends but they struggle to speak up for themselves with the man on the street; others are honest with their partner but find work relationships to be more of a challenge. Wherever you'd like to better please yourself, let the evidence of your unconditional acceptance in the other rings give you the confidence to try.

Remember, this is just a direction of travel; you choose your ultimate destination. For many of my clients, they choose to exercise their acceptance muscles instead when it comes to their families of origin. They make peace with who their parents were and why. They come to terms with, and perhaps grieve for, the aspects of positive parenting they didn't receive and that their parents didn't have to give. They are content to focus their new-found capacity for change on the relationships that occupy their daily lives instead.

It's your journey and it's about identifying where people-pleasing gets in your way and where you want to target your transformation.

Conclusion:
Please Yourself

When it comes to pleasing ourselves, our feelings are our great-est gift. They tell us what we need in any given moment, and how to get it or give it to ourselves.

Without ready access to our own feelings and the all-important permission to act on them, we might have learned to Classic please and end up beholden to the impossibility of perfection, or to Shadow please the ones we perceive as superior, at the cost of our own possibility. We might have worked out how to avoid upset by Pacifier pleasing, keeping the peace without regard for our own integrity. Or we might have got caught in the avoidance of a Resistor, wastefully expending our energy on dodging the pulls to please.

Forsaken feelings

Throughout the stories in this book, we have seen how feelings and needs can be forsaken through people-pleasing. We have seen the damaging impact on the pleasers, as well as on the ones they seek to please. To please ourselves we must learn to recog-nise our feelings and understand what they signal, so that we can take the right steps and feel satisfied, without relying on the warped proxy of people-pleasing. To please yourself, you must be accountable for all your feelings. It means you don't get to choose which ones you want to feel. Either they are all on and you have agency over all of them, or you switch off the painful ones and the joy and meaning of life goes with them, leaving you with the unsatisfactory option of pleasing other people into giving you a version of what you need. If you're lucky.

Being accountable for your feelings means making them matter. It means listening to them with generosity and compassion and acting on them towards a solution that feels validating and representative of your worth. If you've spent your life people-pleasing, this transformation won't happen overnight. It will take time for this part of you that has been neglected to come forwards and trust that you are going to protect and respect it now. I sometimes talk to my recovering people-pleasers about a period of probation ahead. Imagine your feelings as a younger version of you, around six or seven years old. If you want them to tell you their truth, they need to believe that you're not going to criticise or shame them for it. Moreover, they need to believe that there is value in telling you in the first place, that there is reward to justify the risk they'll take in speaking up. If they tell you how they feel and nothing changes, they'll stop trying. The baby who stops crying when left alone again and again hasn't learned how to regulate themselves, they've just learned that there's no point crying if no one ever comes. If you don't come to your own aid, you'll stop feeling too. Earning the trust of your feelings-self might take some patience and practice, and you can bring this process into your awareness by 'checking in' from time to time. Ask yourself, 'What is my relationship with myself like right now? How do I feel, what do I need and how can I get it or give it to myself?' If you find yourself falling back on negative self-talk from your inner critic, step in and stand up for your feelings. As that part of you learns you're on their side, they'll grow in confidence to show up more often, trusting that you'll act on the information and work with them together, as a team, to please yourself.

Health warning

As you begin to unhook from pleasing other people and bring your attention to your own feelings, you'll inevitably have to give up the supply of conditional acceptance and validation that you used to receive from the people you pleased. In this void, things can often feel worse before they feel better. Treat yourself kindly and with compassion and do small positive things for yourself – not because you want to necessarily, or because you think you deserve it yet, but because you need to kick-start your own natural cycle of self-pleasing. Having a list of simple pleasures that's pre-prepared will help you give yourself the attention and reward that you previously earned from other people in exchange for your pleasing services. It's usually easier to come up with joyful things when you're in a good place already, so start by keeping a page open somewhere, in a notebook or on your phone. If you find yourself enjoying a coffee in a particular cafe, jot it down. If you love to take a bath in the middle of the afternoon, add it to the list. Whether it's a running route that makes you feel free, a mug you like to drink from, a song that makes you feel alive, or a podcast guaranteed to lift your spirits, make a note. You don't have to feel like doing any of it when you're feeling low, just pick one and try it out as an experiment. At worst, it won't make a difference. Likely it will help you feel better, not only because of the uplifting thing you did, but because you paid attention to your emotional traffic lights and demonstrated to yourself that you were important enough to validate your feelings and be worthy of your help.

It's not just your own internal critic that you will be up against. There will also inevitably be backlash from the people around you, who are used to you being pleasing. When we set up our relationships to be symbiotic, not everyone will welcome the change. If you start making yourself important and deserving of your own attention, you may be breaking the unwritten rules of your relationship with people who expect you to prioritise their needs. Not everyone will take you up on your offer of authenticity, but the ones who do will be worth it and you can't make an intimacy omelette without breaking symbiotic eggs. Respect your own feelings and take responsibility for your own needs and you'll find that you get the reaction you've been looking for all along – unconditional acceptance from the people who matter and the permission to walk away from those who don't.

The truth hurts sometimes

I was very fortunate to have grandparents in my life who loved me. Every Sunday my brother and I would be dropped off at their house and my grandmother would cook an enormous Sunday roast, making our respective favourite desserts on alternate weeks. We'd turn the television round and watch *Bonanza* re-runs while we ate and, after dinner, Grandad would take us to the corner shop where he'd buy us the plastic guns and chocolate cigarettes that would have been contraband at home. Sometimes he'd drop a coin for us to find and we'd pounce on it gleefully as we walked along, or we'd stop to gorge on black-berries and he'd lift us up to reach the juiciest fruit. One day, I ran across the road towards a particularly tempting crop and he bellowed at me. I burst into tears, heartbroken that my beloved grandfather had shouted. 'I had to shout,' he told me as he consoled me by the side of the road. 'You're too important for me not to.'

That's the truth of pleasing yourself. It's about giving your-self the permission and the freedom to live joyfully, with the caveat that you'll step in with the appropriate protection when it's needed. We don't have to like the protective message, the one that holds us to account for our actions, but we need to care enough about ourselves that we'll listen to it for its wisdom.

Maybe you haven't liked the protective message in this book, the one that tells you to take yourself into account and be responsible for your own needs, instead of outsourcing them to the people you please. Maybe you don't like the message that says not giving a fuck is a cop-out and you need to renegotiate your ambivalent relationship with authority. Maybe you don't like the idea that people-pleasing is manipulative, and I'm not sorry if you don't. I have to tell you the truth, you're too impor-tant for me not to.

The truth is that there are no winners while you're people-pleasing, and as long as you're doing it, you're part of the problem.

The truth is also that you are good enough. In fact, you always were.

For everyone's sake then, Please Yourself.

Acknowledgements

Thank you to 4th Estate and to my wonderful editor, Helen Garnons-Williams, for guiding me with such grace and good humour, and thank you to Charlotte Atyeo for your patience with my penchant for a re-write.

Thank you to my agent, Euan Thorneycroft, and all at A. M. Heath, for your wise counsel and commitment.

Thank you to my best friend, Liz, for being my greatest cheerleader and most trusted advisor. This book would not exist without you, and your unshakeable faith in me.

Thank you to my parents, Keith and Ingrid, and my brother, David, for a lifetime of support and encouragement. I have happy memories of drafting those early chapters on our hotel balcony in the sunshine.

Thank you to my husband, Anton, for always being in my corner.

Thank you to my amazing children, Thomas and Elsa, for being exactly who you are.

Finally, thank you to the late Sarah Grierson who shaped the therapist I am today, and to those important individuals who cannot be thanked by name – my clients.